KU-215-645

RELIGIOUS EDUCATION
AT THE PRIMARY STAGE

RELIGIOUS EDUCATION AT THE PRIMARY STAGE

Ralph R. Gower
with Joanna Daykin, Jo Dewar
and Penny Lewis

LION EDUCATIONAL
Oxford · Batavia · Sydney

Copyright © 1990 Ralph Gower, Joanna Daykin, Jo Dewar and Penny Lewis

Published by
Lion Publishing plc
Sandy Lane West, Oxford, England
ISBN 0 7459 1920 0
Albatross Books Pty Ltd
PO Box 320, Sutherland, NSW 2232, Australia
ISBN 0 7324 0220 4

First edition 1990

British Library Cataloguing in Publication Data

Gower, Ralph
  Religious education at the primary stage.
  1. Primary Schools.
  I. Title
  372.84

ISBN 0-7459-1920-0

Printed and bound in Great Britain
by Cox and Wyman Ltd, Reading

DEDICATION

There is an old saying, a stereotype of course, that behind every successful man there is a woman. In some cases it is absolutely true. This book is written out of the experience I have had as minister, teacher, lecturer, administrator and inspector. But it would not have been possible for me to have so wide and rich an experience without my wife's support. She had to cope when I read for my Master's degree; she had to move with me when I went from job to job, and be there when I worked out my frustrations. And when I was doing two jobs at once, working in the evening at writing, she was willing to forego company so that I could do it. Writing always involves trying out ideas on someone else and when that 'someone else' is a wife who has spent a busy day in a primary school classroom it can be very wearying for her! But she has done all this, and so, in a very real sense, readers who profit from this book owe much to her. I therefore gladly dedicate this book to Margaret, with thanks for making the experience and the book possible.

Ralph R. Gower
London, 1989

CONTENTS

INTRODUCTION

Come with me into a primary school in Newington Green. A group of 7/8 year olds has gone into the library with their teacher and towards the end of the session the teacher asks two children to pick a book for her to read to them all. They choose a book of Bible stories and the teacher begins to read the story of Abraham and Isaac. As she reads there is a protest. 'But that isn't true Miss. It wasn't Isaac. It was Ishmael.' The Turkish Muslim boy knew at once that this was different from what he was told at home. 'Oh no, it wasn't!' Now it was the turn of the Christian children from Greek Orthodox persuasion. The argument went to and fro for a moment until the teacher who was a member of another, quite different, faith asked: 'Who can tell the story as they know it?' And the differences were revealed. Understanding accomplished, the children did not stop there. Where did the stories come from? Where did they learn them? There was no tension, no prejudice. Each child entered into a discussion which led to better understanding of the other.

Or join me for an assembly in Islington. It is springtime and the children are presenting a celebration of spring. They have learned about the spring festivals in many religions and have put on their national costumes to play out and show others how spring features in their community faith. The story of Easter is simply told, as children display artwork they have completed in the classroom. There is music, dance and explanation. The presentation closes with a Jewish boy quietly speaking the blessing he knows from the Synagogue. Everyone listens in quietness and in thanksgiving for the time of inspiration and sharing which they have had.

INTRODUCTION

This is what Religious Education is all about in a County School and in a city where those of different faiths live together with a need for understanding and appreciation of each other. Religious Education is not just a desirable option, however; the Education Reform Act has underlined the statutory nature of RE by writing it into the basic curriculum of every school. It is not an area which many teachers are familiar with as a result of initial training; it is not an area which they can often easily cover in in-service training. This book is written to provide teachers and students with a basic book which meets their needs, and to provide parents and governors with a thorough understanding of what Religious Education at the primary stage is all about.

PART ONE
Primary Religious Education

1

DIRECTIONS FOR RELIGIOUS EDUCATION

When most people speak about Religious Education they think of what goes on in the classroom, because teaching about religions has generally become known as Religious Studies. In fact, Religious Education is much wider and includes assembly. This is because in the days when RE first became a legal requirement RE and assembly were seen as two sides of the same coin, two aspects of the one thing. In the discussions which went on at the time it was suggested that the mind should be engaged in the classroom and the heart should be involved in the hall—a kind of dichotomy between intellect and emotion.

Taking this further some people even used the catch phrase (which has since been out-grown!) that what is 'taught in the classroom is caught in assembly'. As a result the 1944 Education Act put what was called 'Religious Instruction' with 'Collective Worship' to make Religious Education. This does not appear in the formal wording of the Education Act but in the headings of sections 25–30 of the Act. They are headed 'Religious Education in County and Voluntary Schools' and the words go on to say '. . . the school day in every . . . school shall begin with collective worship . . .' (section 25(1)), and 'religious instruction shall be given in every . . . school' (section 25(2)).

We no longer use the phrase 'Religious Instruction' because 'instruction' is too narrow a concept and because it is too close to indoctrination for comfort. In the Education Reform Act 1988 the equation has therefore been changed. It now reads: religious education + collective worship = religious education. There are in fact two different meanings of the 'religious education' element but nobody minds, as long as it is not forgotten that RE and assembly are two parts of the main thing.[1]

RE is locally determined

How is the general direction of RE determined? Who is responsible? In this respect RE is different from all other compulsory elements of the school curriculum. Subject areas in the National Curriculum are designated as 'core' (because they have priority and consist of Mathematics, English, Science and Welsh in Welsh-speaking schools in Wales) or 'foundation' (because they are also very important and consist of History, Geography, Technology, Music, Art, PE, a modern Foreign Language in secondary schools and Welsh in non-Welsh-speaking schools in Wales).

The direction of core and foundation subjects is determined *nationally*. The National Curriculum Council sets out what the Secretary of State for Education and Science wants with specific reference to what targets should be attained by the key ages of 7,11,14 and 16. Although the Secretary of State has personal feelings about this as a reflection of the convictions of the members of his/her political party s/he also listens carefully to the views of those who are involved in education nationally. The direction is reinforced by nationally-determined attainment tests to be administered at 7,11,14 and 16.

RE differs from this. It is still compulsory but the direction is decided upon *locally*, and whether or not there shall be testing at 7,11,14 and 16 is also decided locally, together with the form that such testing will take.

The Agreed Syllabus Conference

The local directions are taken by a body set up by the Local Education Authority called the 'Agreed Syllabus Conference' which is convened to deal with the 'instruction' side of RE. It consists of those sections of the local community who are concerned about and involved in Religious Education. Each section of the local community involved becomes a committee.

One committee is of teachers (preferably including RE teachers) who represent the local Teacher Unions or Associations because teachers are directly involved in teaching from the syllabus.

Another committee represents the Local Education Authority and can consist entirely of elected members, officers (administrators) and/or inspectors (advisers) or a combination of both.

The community as a whole is represented by a Church of England committee (in view of the church's historic involvement in education in this country) and another committee representing 'such Christian and other religious denominations as in the opinion of the Authority will appropriately reflect the principal religious traditions of that area'. This wording, taken from the Education Reform Act, is wider than the 1944 Education Act because although it uses the word 'denomination' which is generally used to designate branches within the Christian Church it is clear that representatives of non-Christian faiths are intended to sit on the committee concerned. This means that if the Authority so decided, this committee would consist of representatives of Christian groups such as Baptists, Methodists, Presbyterians, United Reformed Church members, Quakers, Roman Catholics, Pentecostals and Free Evangelicals: and other faiths such as Buddhists, Hindus, Sikhs, Parsees, Jains, Baha'is, Muslims and Jews. It might be a very large committee and agreement by members might be difficult, but this is the way the law has been framed.

Some people made representations to Government to suggest that instead of Church of England and other-faiths committees there should be Christian and other-faiths committees, but the suggestion was never taken up. Some people would have liked it to have been made clear whether those who had no religious faith could be represented (for example by a Humanist) and, in view of Government's insistence on the importance of parents as governors, whether a parents' committee might not have been better too. It is not impossible, however, for representatives of other groups to become co-opted members on to an Agreed Syllabus Conference: there is nothing in the legislation to forbid this. They might be individual members rather than representative members but their help and views could be given and be of great value.

It does not really matter how large the committees are (except that a very large Conference tends to become unwieldy) because each committee has only one vote on the Conference and decisions about the syllabus have to be unanimous, that is, agreed by a 4–0 vote. This is why the word 'agreement' has become attached to the syllabus so that it is called an 'Agreed' syllabus. In fact there is a further agreement which has to be reached. The syllabus agreed by the four committees in Conference is taken to the Local Education Authority which also has to agree to its use. If agreement at either stage is not possible then the proceedings are taken over by the Secretary of State for Education and Science, who sets up an alternative Agreed Syllabus Conference for the purpose. Since none of the members of a locally-convened Agreed Syllabus Conference wants this to happen there is normally some form of compromise over issues which divide committees.

An example of such compromise features in the Inner London Education Authority syllabus. Surprise has often been expressed that Christianity features so strongly in the ILEA Agreed Syllabus. It states at the outset: 'It is taken for granted that Christianity features clearly.'

It seems strange that the representatives of non-Christian faith groups would support such a statement (although in fact some members of non-Christian faith groups wanted it for cultural reasons). They did so as a result of a compromise, because it was the only way they could make clear that RE would not in any way be a threat to the faith of children in their communities. They wanted the syllabus to say that children might be strengthened in their faith but, because this might have involved indoctrination, in that they never learned about other faiths, they were persuaded to say that they wanted their children to continue in their faith.

The Church of England did not like either form of wording. Members of that committee felt that learning about other faiths carried a risk that a child might not want to continue in his/her own, but the risk was worthwhile because it was possible for faith to be strengthened too.

A compromise was reached. The words enhancing the place of

Christianity would not be opposed by the other-faiths committee if the Church of England would not oppose the aim that children should continue in their own beliefs. So both came within the aim.

It is therefore clear that if a Local Education Authority sets up an Agreed Syllabus Conference which truly reflects the local community then the syllabus itself and Religious Education in general will have a strong local flavour.

This is easily demonstrated historically. The London Syllabus of Religious Education, published in 1947, provides an exclusively Christian syllabus about Christian festivals, Christian stories, Christian biography and Christian prayer, because the community in London at that time was basically Christian.[2] The ILEA syllabus of 1984[3] has a set of primary objectives which do not mention Christianity at all, but religious beliefs, religious ideas, religious concepts, key figures in the various religions and so on, because it is written against the background of a multi-faith community.

It can also be demonstrated geographically. The Agreed Syllabus for Religious Education in Surrey (1987)[4] had no representatives from faiths other than Christianity and, in setting out the content for 5–8 year-olds, children are to be introduced to Christianity through stories, celebrations, people, places and artefacts. They are to understand themselves and others better and to grow more aware of the natural world. The Agreed Syllabus for Waltham Forest (1988)[5] had representatives of Buddhist, Sikh, Jewish, Muslim and Hindu faiths. In the nursery and primary stage objectives there is no mention of Christianity at all. It uses general religious language because it is based upon an aim which includes 'to develop an appreciation of the varieties of religious faith'.

RE syllabuses after the Education Reform Act

The directions taken in the future will be somewhat circumscribed. The new Education Reform Act says that all future Agreed Syllabuses 'shall reflect the fact that the religious traditions in Great Britain are in the main Christian whilst taking account of the teaching and practice of the other principal religions represented in

Great Britain' (section 8(3)). This statement is remarkable for several reasons.

In the debate which preceded the Act there were many Christians in Parliament who wanted to ensure a very strong commitment to Christianity in RE. When I discussed the matter with the Baroness Cox live on *TV-AM* she put forward the view that 80 per cent of RE should be about Christianity—a point I declared to be immoral in the situation where (as in a significant number of ILEA schools) most children are of a non-Christian faith. She later put down an amendment in the House of Lords that RE should be 'predominantly Christian' and when this was not supported by the Bishop of London he was attacked by nine other bishops in a letter to the *Times* which said that Christianity should be central in RE.

The final wording is a long way from the original amendment but it served its purpose. One of the key intentions of members of the Lords and Commons was that Christianity should not disappear. They had grounds for such anxiety. On the one hand there were schools where Christianity had all but disappeared because there was little or no RE in the school, or because Christianity was so 'implicit' that people were not aware of it. On the other hand there were schools where teachers were so strong on the non-Christian faiths in a multi-faith RE situation that Christianity had all but disappeared there too.

The background to this latter situation needs to be understood. ILEA may be cited as a classic example. ILEA primary school teachers up to 1980 had reacted against RE because they identified it with the inculcation of Christianity—indeed they would have said the *indoctrination* of Christianity. It is what they had received when they were at school; it was what they were trained to do (if they received any such training at all) at Colleges of Education. They believed that this was professionally wrong, both in itself and because in a multi-cultural situation it caused problems for children from non-Christian homes.

There was a personal reason for the rejection too, because those teachers who had rejected a personal religious faith had in fact specifically rejected Christianity as their personal religious faith. It is much easier to teach about a faith which has not been personally rejected than one which has!

When multi-faith RE became part of the curriculum in ILEA schools it received wide acceptance because it alleviated the problems which teachers had been facing, but there was still a reluctance to teach about Christianity. This is being overcome as teachers begin to realize that Christianity has many faces as a world faith and that the days of religious indoctrination are gone—at least in the classroom, if not for those in the House of Lords!

What then is required under the new directions for RE? Clearly that Christianity is to be taken seriously and taught properly. This was the intention expressed in debate and it is emphasized in the words 'shall reflect the fact that the religious traditions in Great Britain are in the main Christian'. It is reinforced by the arguments for RE itself.[6] There are many arguments for the inclusion of RE within the curriculum:

● that it gives children understanding about religion so as to minimize misunderstanding and therefore prejudice

● that it gives children opportunity to explore existential questions and find answers which give meaning for their lives

● that it is one of the forms of knowledge or realms of meaning (using the terminology of Hirst and Phenix) without which education is emasculated

● that it is an indispensable component for moral education

● that without it one would be indoctrinating children into humanistic values by neglect . . .

There is also another argument which is of great importance: RE helps children to understand the culture in which they are maturing. Culture is a living thing but there are important historical elements and within those the Christian faith is firmly embedded. Without an understanding of Christianity children cannot fully understand our history, legal system, institutions, customs, literature, art, architecture and so on. No other faith has this kind of influence in Britain.

At the same time as emphasizing Christianity the wording of the Act also emphasizes 'the other principal religions represented in

Great Britain'. They have to be taught properly too. In fact for the first time the law is actually *requiring* multi-faith RE teaching! The national criteria for General Certificate of Secondary Education examinations define the 'major world religions' as 'Buddhism, Christianity, Hinduism, Islam, Judaism, Sikhism' and it is tacitly agreed that this is the meaning of the 'principal religions' phrase in the Education Reform Act.[7] In short, future Agreed Syllabuses have to do justice both to Christianity and to other world faiths.

REFERENCES

[1] This 'equation' will be referred to several times, and to some extent it has to be treated with care. In the DES draft circular on the length and control of schools sessions issued in May 1989, the length of school day for children of different ages is set out. The circular then goes on to say: 'Those hours should include Religious Education; but not the statutory daily act of collective worship . . .' In short a distinction is being made, in fact because Government does not wish governors to think that the act of collective worship will do instead of RE. The point also needs to be made that, in law, headings of a document are not actually part of the law! The headings do, however, reflect the intention of Parliament, which was that RE and collective worship should complement each other.

[2] 'Learning for Life', ILEA, 1968.

[3] 'Religious Education for our Children' (Second edition), ILEA, 1988.

[4] 'The Agreed Syllabus for Religious Education in Surrey', Surrey County Council, 1987.

[5] 'The Agreed Syllabus for Religious Education', London Borough of Waltham Forest, 1988.

[6] These arguments are expanded in the next chapter.

[7] Para 4.3.1 of the GCSE National Criteria for Religious Studies specifies: 'For the purpose of defining content the major world religions shall be Buddhism, Christianity, Hinduism, Islam, Judaism and Sikhism.'

2
AIMS AND OBJECTIVES FOR RELIGIOUS EDUCATION

How do we go about setting an aim for Religious Education? It used to be the fashion for the Agreed Syllabus Conference to set a general aim for Religious Education which summed up all that its members were trying to do in RE. Then everything was fitted to it. It was a good idea because it provided a focus for all that was intended by the time a pupil came to school-leaving age, because for teachers aims are generalized statements of what they hope to achieve by the time the child leaves school. In the provision of a focus it gives direction to what is being attempted.

A clear aim

If we do not know where we are aiming in darts or in archery we are unlikely to hit the target. And without a clear aim, easily kept in mind, the same can happen in Religious Education. Aims do more than this, however.

They provide a means of self-assessment just as the bell that rings on a fair-ground machine to test our strength provides a measure of our physical ability.

They provide motivation, just as the archery butts motivate us to place our arrows in a particular position.

Teachers would say that aims are important because they set out clearly what we want to achieve, enable a teaching task to be analysed, provide a means of evaluation of the teacher's work, challenge the teacher to develop particular skills—and by so doing extend the teacher's performance.

There is another advantage of providing an aim, in the provision of a focus. It sums up the reasons for Religious Education acceptable to the Conference.

Before the ILEA syllabus was produced in 1984 headteachers were approached to see what reasons for RE were acceptable to them. They came up with the arguments which we have already summarized: the 'cultural' argument, the 'world religions (anti-prejudice)' argument and 'existential question' argument. The acceptance of such reasons for RE imply that the content of RE will be related to the reasons. The aim of RE which resulted, therefore, contains all three elements: 'It is taken for granted that Christianity features clearly'; 'to help young people achieve a knowledge and understanding of religious . . . beliefs and practices'; 'to help young people achieve a knowledge and understanding of religious insights'.

As people began to express aims for RE they found that they became complex and the simplicity of aim began to disappear. Suppose we have an aim for our holidays, say, that we want to get to the Isle of Skye. It sets out what we intend, provides a means of evaluation and, if we are driving, encourages the development of particular skills. When we are talking about our plans for our holiday, however, we find that we wish to say more. We might say: 'We're going up to Skye for a holiday so that we can relax and get to know a part of the country we have never been to before, and so that we can come back refreshed for the next round of work.' It is actually quite complex. There is a knowledge and understanding element—'getting to know a part of the country'. There is a personal element—'so that we can relax'. There is a social element—'come back refreshed for the next round of work'.

Many Agreed Syllabuses start with aims of this type. The Manchester Agreed Syllabus (1985) says that the aim of RE is to 'enable pupils to reflect upon and respond to the religious and spiritual beliefs practices insights and experiences that are expressed in human kind's search for meaning in life'. 'Reflect upon' is the cognitive element and 'respond to' can have either a personal or a social reference. The ILEA aim (1984) was a little more complex in saying that the aim is 'to help young people to achieve a knowledge and understanding of religious insights, beliefs and practices so that they are able to continue in or come to their own beliefs and respect the right of other people to hold beliefs different from their own'. The cognitive, personal and social dimensions are perfectly clear in that statement.

Neither the Agreed Syllabus Conference in Manchester nor that in London found such a statement sufficient to describe exactly what was meant. Manchester went on to say that RE was intended to help children and young people to 'develop a knowledge and understanding of the broad cultural religious and spiritual heritage of the entire community and its changing character; . . . fostering in pupils a respect of commitment, beliefs and practices of others . . .' and so on. ILEA needed to write a commentary on the aim which it called 'assumptions'. It said that it was taken for granted that Christianity featured clearly, that RE was not to be confused with political education or social education, that there is no universally agreed definition of religion, and so on.

In other words the factors involved in the formulation of an aim were too many or too complex to generate a simple statement. We shall return to this later, to look at ways in which other Agreed Syllabus Conferences have overcome the problem.

Objectives

Where a clear aim was achieved the next task was to list a set of objectives which would enable the aim to be reached. To go back to our illustration of a holiday in Scotland: the aim of the holiday is to visit the Isle of Skye. There are many objectives which have to be achieved to make this possible. In travelling by road from London, for example, we have to get to the M6 turn-off on the M1; depending what time we start, we may need a lunch-break at Carlisle and a stretch and some tea at Fort William. In addition to this the car has to be reliable, the driver has to be alert and the traffic conditions have to make the journey bearable.

It will be seen at once that there are two kinds of statement here. There are objectives which have to be fulfilled before we can even start to think of progress; but, having achieved them, there are other objectives which register the progress of our journey. It is the same in Religious Education. There are objectives which have to be fulfilled before we can even begin to think about RE.

In the primary school the aims of the school have to be compatible. They should include the development of a child's sense of wonder, appreciation of life, exploration of the world and exploration of relationships. The atmosphere of the school should be such that each child feels secure, is cared for and experiences love and affection. The school must encourage an attitude of respect for one another through accepting the principle that every child, self and others, is important; and that standards and property are to be respected.

In many respects we can say that a prerequisite for Religious Education is simply that the school should be a good primary school: good primary school practice is the necessary condition for good RE. Ron Letheren, the Senior Staff Inspector for Primary RE in ILEA at the time of the formulation of the Agreed Syllabus, wrote a short paper which was incorporated into the Syllabus. He said:

'There are some elements of Religious Education which arise naturally at the primary stage. These derive from the ways that children learn:

Children naturally explore their world; They see the world as a whole and not in separate disciplines of knowledge; They respond to an environment which is well organised, beautiful, stimulating and challenging; Their awareness of standards and integrity is greatly influenced by the example of adults; Children sustain a sense of their own worth and appreciate the worth of others when they themselves are valued and encouraged.

When these ideas pervade the life of the school there should be no difficulty in fulfilling objectives.'

The other objectives are those which become possible in the classroom as a result of the necessary conditions. The ILEA objectives were drawn up by conferences of teachers and although accepted as they stood by the Agreed Syllabus Conference so that the resulting syllabus had the full confidence of teachers, they were never fully satisfactory. The statement of objectives was not internally coherent because it arose from the actual classroom experience of teachers rather than from analysis. Reviewers of the syllabus were quick to point out the deficiencies. Were I to have the opportunity I would want to express them in the following way today:

OBJECTIVES FOR PRIMARY RE

1. To foster children's feelings of awe, wonder, delight and mystery: to assist them in their early exploration of the meaning of life and to help them face and learn from painful experiences which they may encounter such as fear, suffering and death.

2. To encourage children to recognize their own value and importance as individuals, and to promote their social development so that they can give as well as receive.

3. To develop children's understanding that life is a series of significant stages.

4. To help children to consider their personal response to moral issues.

5. To introduce children to the lives of key figures in various religions and to people who have responded to their teaching and example by telling the stories which have been written about them.

6. To give children the experience and language which will help them to develop religious concepts and understanding of the religious beliefs held by other people.

7. To familiarize children with sacred books and the stories which they contain.

8. To stimulate in children a curiosity about and a search for knowledge about worship, ritual, festival and other expressions of religious life and practice.

9. To develop skills in children—such as music, movement, art and craft—so that they are able to respond to religious ideas which have been transmitted in such forms and, where appropriate, express their own feelings in such form.

10. To help children develop the confidence to express their own beliefs and ideas about religion and listen to others.

Types of objective

It would be possible to work through the list of objectives in detail. They are, however, given as an example of what can be done, rather than as a prescription to be followed. Nevertheless there are some very important points to be made. It will be noted that the objectives are of different kinds.

The ones most obviously connected with RE are numbers 5–8. These involve stories of the lives of founders and followers, religious language and experience to help children to form concepts about religion, the contents of sacred books, festivals and ritual. Because they are obviously religious in content they are normally referred to as *explicit RE objectives*. They are things to which the adjective 'religious' can be applied.

The first four objectives do not look like Religious Education at all to many people; they are simply things which might be expected in any primary school. They are not, however, the same as the prerequisites for Religious Education we recently looked at. They are objectives for the classroom which are an extremely important part of Religious Education. They provide the language and experience which give meaning and relevance to the explicitly religious objectives and they cannot be separated from them.

How can a child understand why a Jewish boy child is circumcized (objective 8) without knowing something of the significant stages of life (objective 3)?

How can children begin to understand the Christian teaching about salvation (objective 6) without recognizing their own value and importance as an individual (objective 2)?

What has sometimes been called *implicit RE* is providing

language and experience which makes it possible for Religious Education to take place. What makes it Religious Education is the intention. When teachers contrive an experience or utilize the situation which has arisen for teaching purposes, because they know that this will help the child's Religious Education then it is Religious Education. RE does not happen by accident. The importance for RE of the first four objectives (or similar ones) is that the teacher plans for them and prepares for them. They are not simply left to chance, and it is not assumed that RE is happening in the 'general ethos of the school' or in the 'standard good practice' in the classroom.

We must also look at objectives 9 and 10 which are different. They relate to skills rather than to understanding of content. RE is very heavily content-laden because religion is a very large field of study, but it does not simply deal with content. The self-expression of religion through the arts is a very important dimension and all the knowledge in the world would be of little use without the ability to communicate.

Implicit RE

I have often found that Christian parents are worried about the idea of implicit Religious Education. Too many parents have claimed that implicit RE is watered-down RE. This perception has arisen partly because of misunderstanding by some parents and partly because of misunderstanding by some teachers. When we use the word 'implicit' in a general way (not technical RE) we are saying that something is 'hidden' in something else. Love is implicit in willingness to go to the shops for mum. Many teachers (who had not received specialist RE training) heard the phrase 'implicit RE' and assumed that it meant that RE was 'hidden' in something else—in the moral standard of the school for example, or in the way that people related, and so on. They therefore assumed that they were doing the RE which was required of them within the ethos of the school. They got it wrong, and because they got it wrong RE did become diluted into attitudes and ethos within the school. Where this has happened a proper understanding is needed so that things are put right. Parents had every right to show their concern.[1]

Christian parents need not be concerned about genuine 'implicit RE' simply because they cannot see it. They may need reminding that the foundations of a house cannot normally be seen, but the walls cannot go up without them. Invisible foundations do not mean that there is a weakness. Furthermore they need to realize that the Bible recognizes implicit RE as well as explicit RE. It does not use these terms, but theologians refer to 'natural revelation' where God is revealed in the universe, in history and in conscience and 'special revelation' where God reveals himself personally.

In Psalm 19 David was able to say, 'the heavens declare the glory of God and the firmament proclaims his handiwork.' In Romans 2 Paul was able to say, 'what can be known of God is plain to (us) because God has shown it to (us). Ever since the creation of the world, his eternal power and deity have been clearly perceived in the things which have been made.' Natural revelation is followed by special revelation, just as implicit RE is followed by explicit RE.

Christians might also consider the example of Jesus. He very seldom started with special revelation from the 'Bible' of his day. He started from the ordinary experience of a shepherd, a farmer, a woman who lost part of her wedding gift, the king going on a journey and people waiting to be hired for work in a vineyard. In fact Christian parents who yearn for a diet of Bible stories for their children might do well to remember that the reason for the emphasis on Bible stories in RE in the past is not a comfortable one.

When the 1944 Education Act had made RE statutory, and it came into force, Christians were so bound by their denominations that they did not trust RE teachers to teach about Christianity without influencing children to join a particular kind of church. About the only thing that was considered 'safe' was Bible stories and early church history! What Christians actually believed or how they expressed that belief was 'out'. We have, mercifully, overcome the lack of trust and it is now possible for children to learn about what Christians believe and how they express their faith. Of course the Bible is part of Religious Education. It is essential for Christians in the same way as all Scriptures are vital to followers of the faith.

But children can learn about Christianity and are no longer limited to Bible stories.

Confusion of objectives

Now let us return to the aim of Religious Education. We said earlier that simple aims became complex because there were a large number of things which needed to be said about Religious Education. Statement of aim was in one case supported by a commentary and was always related to a set of objectives. The problem with aim and objectives is that the objectives are of different kinds and this is confusing when there are a large number of objectives. There were an increasing number of objectives, too, as people began to understand more about Religious Education, understood more of its potential, and needed to set down exactly what was involved so that parents and teachers would know what was expected.

It became fashionable in curriculum terms to analyse objectives into knowledge, skills and attitudes and this is what many Agreed Syllabus Conferences have attempted to do in RE. In fact this was not as simple as it seemed.

Many Agreed Syllabus Conference members were not at all sure what was intended by knowledge. Durham (1980), copied by Sheffield (1986), uses the word 'concept' instead of knowledge and analyses the concept objectives as those which contribute to the idea of a spiritual dimension to life and those which contribute towards the idea of religious approach to life. Surrey (1987) noted that knowledge objectives involved learning (acquiring and record-ing information), understanding and evaluating, presumably influenced by the criteria which were being used in the new GCSE examinations. Waltham Forest (1987) felt that knowledge was represented by experience as well as concepts.

Worse, there seemed to be a confusion between knowledge, skills and attitudes. Salford put 'understanding of characteristic use of language and literary forms in religious books' as a skill. But 'understanding of themselves and their personal qualities' was put as a value, and 'understanding of people and the relationships with them' was put under exploration of human experience. Durham put 'understanding and sharing experiences of awe and wonder' as a skill; Cambridge as part of exploration and reflection on human experience, quite distinct from skills.

An examination of syllabuses produced in the 1980s will show considerable agreement about the area of RE but disarray over terminology used to analyse it. The following diagram may help.

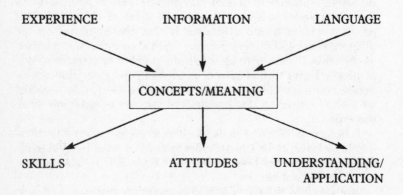

This indicates that it is the intention of the RE syllabus to provide children with experience, information and language so that they can form concepts or areas of meaning. Whether the concepts have been fully achieved can be ascertained by assessment which centres on skills, attitudes and understanding. Whether such a model for sorting out the confusion will be acceptable will remain to be seen, as at the time of writing the whole issue is one of vigorous debate. The interesting thing is that most RE specialists are agreed on the concepts or 'concept clusters' which lie at the heart of Religious Education. One list set out by GCSE working parties suggested 7: symbol, authority, belief, value, ultimate questions, lifestyle and (underlying them all) spirituality.[2]

What is often not understood is that there are different levels of concepts. A concept is a shorthand word which combines several ideas into one.

Let us imagine a banana, apple, pear, orange, melon and grapefruit. We describe them as fruit. Fruit is a concept and it saves us having to use all the individual words when we are talking about them. Suppose we now take a list of words similar to and including fruit: meat, fish, vegetables, cake, cereals. We describe them as food. 'Food' is a higher-order concept than 'fruit' because it cannot be understood until the concept of 'fruit' is grasped. If we put food together with water, air, warmth and protection we would be talking about a still higher order of concept, necessities of life of which food is simply a sub-concept.

The aim of Religious Education is to provide a series of relevant experiences, pieces of information and language which will lead to higher, and higher-order concepts about religion.[4] Salvation might be part of the area of belief but pupils are not going to be able to understand salvation until they have learned what it is to be saved, not in a religious way but in all kinds of other ways—to be saved from drowning by a lifeboat, to save each week and put in the Bank, and to feel safe and tucked up for the night.

With the advent of the Education Reform Act, core and foundation subjects are to have targets set for the end of 7, 11, 14 and 16 years and tasks are to be devised to see how well children have come up to the targets. There is great discussion whether this should or should not be done in Religious Education. Some people do not like the idea of assessment in RE, because surely religion deals with things which cannot be assessed? To assess therefore distracts from the spirituality element of RE. But a realistic view is that unless there is assessment RE will succumb to pressure from the other subjects where assessment is required. If parents judge schools by their levels of achievement and place their children in the schools which show highest levels of achievement, and if school governors under the Local Management of Schools scheme are paid to run the school on the basis of a formula related to the number of pupils in the school, then the headteacher has to give all the time possible to those subjects which will be assessed. If RE is not assessed, it will be squeezed out. RE staff will therefore have to work out what concepts are possible at the ages of 7 and 11, and what experiences, information and language will be necessary to achieve them.

REFERENCES

[1] There is even more confusion about 'implicit'. Edward Bailey runs a society studying 'implicit religion' which is basically the study of folk religion.

[2] Secondary Examination Council: Report of Working Party—Religious Studies—Draft Grade Criteria (1987?) para: 2.4.

[3] The working party was within the ILEA producing material to help teachers in secondary schools to cope with profiling and records of achievement. It is not available outside of ILEA.

[4] We must not forget that concepts are also clarified. Some children start with a general idea of food, and later come to an understanding of what food is. This is dealt with later in Chapter 3.

ACTIVITIES

● Write out your own aim for RE and provide a commentary to explain why you have written it as you have.
● Critically evaluate the 10 objectives set out in this chapter.

3

RELIGIOUS EDUCATION IN THE CLASSROOM

Once we know the thrust, direction or aim of Religious Education it is necessary to set down and work out how this is to be achieved with a particular group of children in a particular place. Decisions for a County School will not be the same as decisions for a family, a religious community or even a Voluntary (Aided) School. The purpose of Religious Education in a County School is to educate children about religion or religions: the purpose in a family might be to induct children into the faith, so that at a particular time they are converted or become committed to the faith—to teach so that they become believers.

This does not mean that community and school are opposed to each other. Rather, they complement each other. The school supplies information and understanding. The community utilizes that knowledge, and adds to it, in a way which leads the child in the desired direction. Where the trust deeds of a Voluntary (Aided) School are constituted to encourage children to come into and express a particular faith, the Religious Education, assembly and voluntary group might also be used to this end. It is important to note that this not true of every Voluntary (Aided) School. As most of these schools are church schools, it can be said that although some church schools were founded to bring children up into the beliefs and practices of the Church of England, for example, others were set up as the outworking of Christian concern for the local community—to provide children with a good all-round education where, otherwise, they would have had none.

When we determine a programme of work for a particular school, or a smaller group of children, we normally refer to it as a 'scheme of work'. In primary schools, at class level, this is sometimes referred to as a 'forecast'. The essential thing is that work has to be planned. In planning for Religious Education, within the constraints of the aim incorporated into the Agreed Syllabus, there are a number of very important balances which have to be held.

BALANCE OF CONTENT—1

Let us go back to the arguments put forward for having Religious Education on the curriculum. The following is a brief summary:

● **The world faiths argument.** Religion has a very important place in the world. Most people are religious. Religious people feel very deeply about their beliefs to such an extent that at some times, and in some places, it has led them into conflict. As the world has become smaller, due to developments in travel and communication, people are becoming aware of each other's faiths and in many of the world's cities people of different faiths are living close together. It is therefore important to gain understanding of each other's faiths so as to avoid misunderstanding and pre-empt the possibility of prejudice and conflict.

● **The cultural argument.** All children grow up into a culture. Language, history, traditions, beliefs, attitudes to life, style of dress are the things which make a particular group distinct and distinctive. Children need to understand the culture they are growing up into in order to find their way as people. Religion is often one of the most important elements of a culture. Therefore children need to understand the place that religion has had, and/or has, in their own culture in order to arrive at understanding and maturity. Although culture is a living thing and a changing thing, it is still true that Christianity has an important place in British culture. We cannot properly understand British history, customs, institutions, law, art, literature, architecture . . . without understanding something of Christianity.

Before we go on we need to stop and recognize that these points seem to be reflected in the Education Reform Act which requires both Christianity and other world religions to be taught about properly.

If there are curriculum arguments for RE it follows that Religious Education will address itself to giving information and understanding about all world religions including Christianity. The cultural argument has already made it clear that religion concerns many other areas of life. This means that, although distinct in its own right, Religious Education also has links with many other areas of the curriculum. It would not be possible to study art comprehensively without reckoning on the importance of religious art; it would not be possible to become involved in dance without realizing the importance of dance in religion. But knowledge and understanding of religious traditions, though important elements of RE, are not the whole picture . . .

● **The existential argument.** At the root of life there are fundamental questions: 'Who am I?', 'Why am I here?', 'Where am I going?', 'What is the purpose of life?' and 'What happens when my life comes to an end?'. Answers to these questions give meaning to life. If we do not have answers to these questions, life has no meaning and, when we are under stress, we 'crack up' or 'go to pieces'. A knowledge of answers to these questions keeps us whole.

Questions of this kind are introduced in Religious Education because they lie at the heart of all religions, and as children become aware of the questions they become aware of the answers which have been given and they begin to find answers for themselves. This search for meaning and purpose is one of the key elements of Religious Education and it follows that time should be allocated in RE lessons for this search to take place.

Many people would restrict the purpose and content of Religious Education to these two dimensions—a knowledge and understanding of religious traditions and a search for meaning and purpose in life. The ILEA syllabus, for example, shows that this is the case in Inner London. The syllabus starts by giving these reasons for Religious Education under the heading 'Why Religious Education is Important' and immediately goes on to express the reasons in an aim. But there are other arguments which may be put forward for Religious Education.

● **The 'liberal education' argument.** There are many ways of looking at the world in which we live. We can look at it scientifically to seek reasons for what happens and to formulate laws which demonstrate how things hang together. In doing this we develop characteristic styles of working and a vocabulary which enables us to work within this category.

But scientific method is only one way of looking at the world. There is a moral way of looking at the world; scientific experiment cannot measure whether something is right or wrong. There is an aesthetic way of looking at the world; science cannot measure the degree of beauty in a sunset. There is a historical way of looking at the world and so on. Each way of looking at the world has its own unique ideas, approaches and vocabulary. These have been identified as 'forms of knowledge' by Hirst and 'realms of meaning' by Phenix. Each individual is unique and the more ways a person has of looking at the world, or at reality, it is argued, the richer that person's life has the potential to become. One of the unique ways of looking at reality is through religion. It has its own approaches, such as faith, its own vocabulary and its own unique ways of expression. It is argued that if a child does not learn the religious approach to life then he or she will be deprived of one of the ways to view the world.

If this argument is accepted, it again makes a difference to the material we are teaching. Religion has to be shown to be unique—a completely different, but valid, way of looking at the world in which we live.

● **The moral argument.** It has always been clear that people have linked moral objectives with Religious Education. In the debates which preceded the 1944 Education Act, about incorporating religion into the curriculum, it was said by some Members of the House of Commons that, if children learned Christianity, Europe might be saved from future evils akin to Nazism. Similar sentiments were expressed in the debates which preceded the 1988 Education Reform Act. It was suggested that we might be saved from 'football hooliganism' and 'crimes of violence' if Religious Education was strengthened in the new Act. Many Muslim leaders have allowed their children to learn about Christianity because of the strong links between Islam and Christianity in the moral field. But the subtle relationship between Religious Education and morality has been misunderstood in the debate.

Some elements of Religious Education (but not all) do involve Moral Education. When children learn about the founders, leaders and followers of world religions they study the teachings of these figures. Such teachings often lead to the observation that human life needs to be valued and that other people need consideration—an important aspect of Moral Education. When, however, children learn about the features of a religious building, Moral Education is not necessarily involved.

Some elements of Moral Education (but not all) do involve Religious Education. When children look at the reasons for moral behaviour it is not possible to leave out a religious element. While motives sometimes involve personal opinion, consensus or philosophical belief, for some people the motive to act morally involves religious belief. When moral questions arise in learning about the progress of medical science, it is unprofessional to discuss the issue without reference to religious standpoints. When, however, children learn about the Hedonist belief that right is what brings pleasure, or when they look at psychological explanations of morality, Religious Education will not normally be involved.

The curriculum areas are, therefore, quite distinct but there is some overlap. A similar distinction exists between Moral Education and other curriculum areas. Moral Education is much more important in the life of the school and in its general ethos. It is only when people are treated as individuals—as people who are significant—that they begin to realize the importance of treating others in the same way. It is only when there is consistency of standards, rather than inconsistency and chaos, that children begin to learn the desirability of consistency. It is only when relationships between staff are governed by high standards that children learn to value high standards. Those of us involved in RE are grateful when the inseparable relationship between religion and morality is underlined. However, if Moral Education is undermined by, say, poor personal relationships in the school, Religious Education is not to be blamed. The curriculum links between ME and RE have been noted; if the argument is accepted it follows that there will be a moral input or a clear moral strand within the RE teaching programme.

● **The indoctrination argument.** We looked earlier at the contention that since religion is a unique way of looking at reality, failure to help children to have a religious perspective is to cut them off from a whole area of human experience, thus leaving them deprived. The 'indoctrination' argument is similar. It argues that if children are not taught about religions the curriculum puts across a hidden message that religion is unimportant (because it cannot be said that religion does not exist).

Some people have made the point that religion might be too important to include in the school curriculum and should be restricted to home and community. It does not, however, work out this way. Children in school recognize that they are dealing with every aspect of life. If religion is omitted from the teaching programme it indicates that it is left out for a particular reason— that it is not truly educational.

Children entering reception class will already have had experience of relationships. They know what is regarded as right and wrong for them. They will have been involved in celebrations and (depending on their home background) they might have been involved in distinctly religious experiences. They will have been involved in sorrow and loss and they will have been helped to cope with it. Totally to deny these experiences, by refusing to have RE in the curriculum, is a positive reinforcement of secularistic values and a powerful means of inducting children into a secularist philosophy. If children do not understand that there is a religious/spiritual dimension to life they will be indoctrinated into secularistic beliefs because the general thrust of contemporary society is consumerist and secularist. In fact great care has to be taken to ensure that the very approach taken in teaching Religious Education is itself not affected by secularism.

At one time a study of world religions was described as a 'Cook's Tour' or 'Taking what we wanted from the shelves of a religious supermarket'. Such descriptions are not dead and still live on in arguments put forward for the study of a strictly limited number of world religions. These arguments are forwarded on the grounds that there is likely to be confusion and tokenism if all world religions are dealt with. The importance of the 'supermarket' approach is not the variety of religions on offer (after all our aim is to make children religiously literate, not give them a total understanding of all world religions!) but the assumption that through purely intellectual assessment a religion can be chosen for oneself. Such a view is a thoroughly secularist one!

Most religions believe in revelation. In the Christian faith, for example, it is clear in the New Testament that humankind is unable to choose God, because basic human nature does not wish to make such a choice. It is therefore necessary for God to overcome our ignorance and obtuseness and in the end choose us. Divine revelation must 'break in' in order that we can know. The idea that we can, as it were, stand above and beyond religion and choose in a purely cerebral way is alien to much religious thought. When we face this in thinking through the balances for our RE material, not only do we have to ensure that religious material is not squeezed out, but we have also eventually to come to the point where pupils will be able to understand philosophies such as secularism, and its ally humanism, properly to evaluate its effect on our thinking.

INDOCTRINATION AND SECULARISM

It is worthwhile digressing at this point with something of a wry smile, because it is normally the secularists who use the idea of indoctrination as an argument against religion and Religious Education.

In fact the whole thrust of thinking about indoctrination is secularist in style. Although the term tends to be used to describe a form of communication which one personally dislikes and therefore becomes a 'boo' word, it is much more than this.

Indoctrination is a way of presenting ideas or information in a way that, through the bias, selectivity or influence of the presenter, the ideas are received and accepted although they may not otherwise have been acceptable. The influence of the presenter may cause someone to accept beliefs on non-rational grounds ('the teacher says so'). The bias of the presenter may lead to decisions being taken when only part of the truth was made available. The careful selection of materials by the presenter may fail to reveal that the matter is controversial. The acceptance may lead to a closed mind. But indoctrination is more than this.

Indoctrination involves putting a person at a disadvantage when judged from the standpoint of rational human beings. What do we mean by disadvantage? It is this which lies at the heart of achieving an understanding of indoctrination. It is probably impossible for all of the elements which are needed for a totally informed decision to be brought together but, in essence, indoctrination occurs when the known truth is consciously withheld in order to persuade someone to come to a particular viewpoint, so putting them at a disadvantage.

So indoctrination is the communication of ideas in a way which bypasses critical faculties and imposes pressure through personality or through the manipulation of emotions to put someone at a disadvantage.

It is perfectly acceptable to encourage children to have set ideas in such areas as consideration for others, but it is indoctrination when children are encouraged to have closed minds on matters of debate. All this seems fairly straightforward until we ask, 'By what criteria should a position of disadvantage be assessed?', 'By what criteria should closed minds be judged?'.

Judgment should be made from the standpoint of rational humankind, which is of course a humanistic perspective! This is why the criteria for indoctrination are the subject of fierce debates. Indeed, by its own terms, it would be a form of indoctrination were this not to be made clear. The debate is particularly fierce between Humanists and religious believers. Muslim parents, for example, consider it essential that children have closed minds to other faiths, in the sense that they must not consider them as viable options. Christians would say that it is not controversial at all that Jesus Christ was 'crucified, dead and buried, and on the third day he rose again'. If therefore we take a definition of indoctrination which does not recognize how controversial that definition is, and if we declare emotionally for the importance of rationality, we could actually be indoctrinating pupils into the principles of rationalism. The way to avoid this is to be open about this matter along with others.

BALANCE OF CONTENT—2

If teachers prepare a scheme of work which is matched to the reasons for RE they should get a balanced result. Similarly, if the reasons for RE are expressed in an overall aim, and the aim is expressed through a series of objectives related to each age group, and these are used to produce a scheme of work, there should also be a balanced result. In fact the results should be the same! Experience shows, however, that teachers find it easier to work with a series of objectives than they do with a rationale for RE—probably because the objectives are more 'finely tuned'. It is therefore necessary to look at the objectives and ensure that our teaching holds each in balance. Let us look at the objectives for RE which we summarized earlier. We can give them titles:

Peak Experiences
Identity
Development
Moral Issues

Religious People
Religious Language and Ideas
Religious Stories
Religious Activities

Understanding Communication
Self-expression

We have already noted that these titles fall into three groups— implicit, explicit and skills objectives. We have to make sure that all of the groups, and each of the objectives within a group, actually feature in our scheme of work.

Implicit objectives

The implicit RE which we have discussed earlier comes through a number of experiences. Peak experiences are those which 'turn people on' to religion. They arise through awe and wonder, excitement and reverence, sorrow and loss—any experience which opens up the fundamental questions of human existence such as 'Why am I here?' It is important that children know what these experiences are.

There is a sense in which these questions have importance right across the curriculum. If children do not receive unified, positive images about themselves they will not grow into healthy integrated adults. A boy who receives a message that he is valued and important at home, but at school receives a message that he is a nuisance and a troublemaker, will have problems in reconciling the images. If the pictures children get of themselves are inconsistent or if these pictures are all negative, children will feel they are dirty, useless, worthy of punishment and unintelligent. Some children will live up to the image, some will fight it and become aggressive, others will accept it and withdraw into themselves. This whole area of contradictory messages becomes particularly important for children of a minority faith group in a majority Christian culture or for Christian children in a majority materialistic culture.

If children are made to feel that they do not count, that their faith is undervalued, that their parents who taught them their faith are ignorant and wrong in their approach to life, they may lose the opportunity to become fully integrated people. The teacher, therefore, has to ensure that the child's personality develops in an integrated way. The teacher who has regard for human personality will not treat a child in any other way. But it goes beyond this.

Each religious faith puts a particular value upon the child within their community—either at one extreme, where the individual is all-important, or at the other where the community is all-important. There are often particular religious ceremonies linked with the development of the individual that mark a child's development in birth, maturity and marriage. The rites associated with this passage are referred to as 'rites of passage'. These signify the critical points in life when the help of one's God is of crucial importance. Only as children become conscious that they are individuals who will change and grow will such ceremonies have any meaning.

Moral issues raise other basic 'Why?' questions—'Why does my baby sister lose her temper?' 'Why am I always picked on at school?' 'Why are there floods in Bangladesh?' 'Why did grandpa have to die?' These questions tend to be raised by children as things happen to them. So it is difficult to plan for them unless the issues come through in stories. Provided that the nature of implicit RE is understood, the teacher is unlikely to go overboard on the matter. It was the mistaken belief that RE took place almost exclusively through implicit RE—interpreted as ethos, Moral Education, caring and sharing—which led to such an emphasis on the implicit. In addition, teachers were often nervous of explicit RE.

Explicit objectives

Now that RE teaching has become much more 'objective' explicit teaching about religions has become more common. Children need to learn about founders of religions and about their followers so that they become aware of the living, contemporary nature of faith. It is possible to bring out the differences in the founders and in the nature of their beliefs through stories of the people concerned. Festival days linked to stories of the founders are obvious opportunities for doing this. Children need to learn through story the important part that religion plays in many people's lives. Stories have a wider purpose than simply telling stories of people. Story-telling has been used to communicate faith, to challenge and inspire and to enable ideas to be easily remembered. A story recalled in adulthood will bring further insight into what lies behind the tale. Stories are so important in religion that we need to stop for a moment and look at them in greater detail. However, stories should not be used indiscriminately.

Joan Cass[1] suggests that stories should be selected for their plot, content and theme, characterization, style and format.

SELECTION OF STORIES

1. Plot

Does the book tell a good story? Is it believable at either the imaginative or the reality level? Is there action and suspense, however simple? Is it plausible and credible without relying on coincidence and contrivance?

2. Content and theme

Is the story appropriate for the age and the stage of development for which it has been designed? Is the story worth telling? Does it avoid moralizing and yet help to give children a sense of values and purpose? Do truth and justice prevail?

3. Characterization

Are the characters real and convincing? Can their strengths and weaknesses be seen—particularly in stories for older children who are able to see that people are neither wholly good nor wholly bad? Has the author avoided types? Do the characters develop and grow?

4. Style

Does the style fit the story and the subject matter? Is it clear and understandable, with dialogue suitable to the characters? Is there an exciting and imaginative use of words and a richness of expression?

5. Format

Is the appearance of the book attractive? Does it have print appropriate for the intended age group? Is it durable, with good quality paper and strong binding? Do the illustrations add to its attraction, echoing and enhancing the story and stimulating children's imagination and curiosity? If it is meant to provide children with real information, is it accurate in text and illustration?

There are a number of criteria which should be used in connection with religious stories. Stories which inappropriately emphasize the frightening, cruel and ugly should be avoided. The word 'inappropriately' is deliberately used. Many writers in the RE field recommend that, as well as omitting stories of harsh punishment, judgment and the end of the world, the theme of the crucifixion should also be avoided. This appears to be unrealistic. Apart from the fact that young children, through the media, are conscious of violent death, the crucifixion is too central to the Christian faith to be omitted. It is part of almost any child's normal experience, as a symbol in churches and at Easter. Elements of the story of the crucifixion can be made known therefore, without dwelling too much upon elements which would do harm.

Stories which involve adult themes and relationships and those of other cultures and faiths which stereotype, or make false generalizations, should also be avoided. Stories involving miraculous events should be told only with careful presentation. In telling such stories, teachers must realize the danger of emphasizing the supernatural element at the expense of the point or message of the story.

MIRACLE STORIES

An additional note needs to be made about miracle stories.

Some teachers argue that miracle stories should be avoided altogether at this stage because:

● Miracles are to be understood in a theological context which is beyond children

● Some miracles are regarded by some Christians as symbolic, and the symbolism cannot be understood by children

● At this stage, identification of miracle stories with the fantasy world of infancy could lead to a rejection of the story and its meaning when the fantasy stage is passed.

There is, however, another side to the argument. The three objections are based upon a hierarchy of learning skills (distinguishing fantasy from reality; understanding the symbolic; understanding the intervention of the personal; understanding the nature of scientific law) instead of starting with the story itself.

An alternative way of approaching miracle stories is to learn about them as stories at infant level and to follow this up with appropriate insights into their meaning at the right ages and stages. Supporters of this approach believe that the anxieties of their colleagues are based upon a confusion between telling stories and the development of (say) mathematical skills.

Another reason for telling miracle stories is that they are part of our literary heritage and should not be left until too late.

This is not an argument for or against telling miracle stories, rather a recommendation that they should be told only after careful consideration.

We have looked at the different types of story which are part of Religious Education, and at a means of selecting them. We turn finally to look at how stories should be told. There are four basic pieces of advice:

● Normally tell; do not read, even if the book is held to provide a focus. Not only does this prevent problems of unsuitable vocabulary/sentence length and so on but, by watching the children, there is immediate feedback about problems and misunderstanding.

● Prepare for telling the story to ensure that words are simple and sentences short, and that anything children should not hear is removed.

● Follow the story with questions to increase understanding and reinforce details.

● If books are used, they should be used occasionally; pictures should be good and large enough to be shown to the children. Books are useful to reinforce the story, particularly with older infants.

The role of story is clearly of great importance in RE. But as well as learning about key personalities, events and things of significance in religion through stories, children will need to learn about things that religious people do—how they worship, what rituals they follow, what festivals are celebrated and what they believe. This is not something that will happen all at once; there is growth in conceptualization.

As children become more familiar with language and ideas so their ability to understand concepts grows and early confusions are sorted out. Children will learn, for example, that 'red' is differentiated into crimson, scarlet and magenta, 'aeroplane' becomes specifically Boeing, BAC and ATP. This is important because some people have claimed that teaching children about several religions causes confusion. However, this will depend, not on the number of religions studied, but on the child's motivation. How many junior age children are confused by the team colours and league positions of football clubs? Are children confused by the names of countries and the stamps which they issue? Not normally; in fact a detailed knowledge of lists and facts is characteristic of many primary age children. Words and facts are collected and treasured in the same way as dolls in national costume or model cars. Explicit RE has a very important place in the teaching of religion but it has to be balanced against and with implicit RE.

Skills objectives

There has been a strong emphasis in RE on content—knowledge and understanding. The remaining objectives remind us that skills are important too. Religion is communicated through language, but also through the performing and expressive arts.

It is only as children gain confidence through self-expression and learn to show their understanding of, and feelings about, religion that they can learn to express themselves through the arts. By doing this they begin to understand the communication of religion through, for example, Christian symbol, Hindu drama and Islamic calligraphy. There are skills which arise in other areas of the primary curriculum that are also essential for RE. Children must develop skills that can be used to control and direct their own learning. Some skills, like learning to read and using a dictionary, are clearly shared with all other subjects, but entering imaginatively into other people's experiences is shared mainly with the humanities.

It is as well to remember that the balance of objectives may change as the child gets older. Implicit objectives often feature more strongly at the infant stage than at the junior stage. At the infant stage we are especially concerned with the extension of experience, the development of identity and relationships, appreciation of the physical world, learning sensitivity, expressing creativity, celebrations and stories. Later we become especially concerned with biographies, artefacts, sayings, writings, visits, language (the visible side of religions), primarily with reference to those religions which are visible locally.

BALANCE BETWEEN CONTRIVED AND CAPITALIZED EXPERIENCES

If we were to look at a list of the experiences children should have, the information they should be given, and the language they should learn truly to fulfil the aims of RE we would see that some of these experiences would have to be planned for but that others would happen anyway.

RELIGIOUS EDUCATION IN THE CLASSROOM

Children will encounter at least some of these experiences as they grow up:

- A favourite pet will die
- Special treats will be given by adults
- Birthdays will take place
- Classroom discipline will raise matters of right and wrong
- A playground quarrel will lead to reconciliation
- Items of international news will involve world religions
- Events such as a state funeral or the visit of a religious leader will be seen on television
- Weddings will happen in the family and birth celebrations will take place
- Religious buildings might be passed on the way to school
- Food relating to religious festivals will be seen in local shops
- Some children will be involved in religious celebrations at home.

It is important to capitalize on experiences of this kind which arise from children's natural interests and activities at home. The teacher should expect such things to happen, be prepared and make space in the scheme of work for them, so that it is clear that these experiences are not going to be omitted. Indeed, it is essential that they do happen as experiences of this kind often provide information, experience and insights into areas of which the teacher may have little personal experience.

The child who takes part in an elder sister's wedding, is able to describe what happens, and bring things to school is a valuable resource. The only danger is that the information may not always be accurate, but parents are normally only too willing to help. One helpful way of capitalizing on a situation is to use educational television programmes. Many of these programmes are excellent for RE purposes. Where teachers find their expertise is wanting they can learn much from the TV programmes and handbooks.

Once such areas of experience are identified it is possible to list other areas of experience which are not so likely to happen 'by chance'. Teaching about a charity, writing about feelings of fear when going home in the dark, learning stories about the life of the prophet Muhammad, visiting the local Methodist Church,

49

handling a Jewish scroll, finding out about fasting during the month of Ramadan, watching an Indian dancer, or writing about the blind person who spoke in assembly, are all things which the teacher can organize in order to balance those things which will happen anyway. Both are necessary. Without the planned approach it is too easy to leave things to chance and opportunities may be missed. Without the approach which capitalizes on opportunities it is possible to divorce religion from real life.

We now need to look in more detail at the whole issue of how children actually come to an understanding of religious concepts. Two questions arise:

● Will children get muddled by learning about different religions?

● Are some religious ideas too complex for children?

We covered the first question when we discussed clarification of concepts. The second question cannot be dealt with properly unless we look back to the history of the theory of RE—to the 1960s when Ronald Goldman enquired into 'Readiness for Religion'.

Goldman was aware that the RE of his day had failed in the areas of knowledge and understanding. Tests taken by children who had undergone a Bible-centred course in primary and secondary schools revealed that their knowledge and understanding of the subject was minimal. Goldman knew from the work of Swiss psychologist Jean Piaget that children had to pass through distinct stages of thinking if they were to come to a mature understanding. Using Piaget as his inspiration Goldman devised experiments which seemed to show that there were distinct stages in the development of religious thinking.

● At the first stage—the pre-operational stage—children use themselves as a centre of reference, can attend to only one thing at a time and cannot look back on their train of thought. Their understanding of religion, therefore, is very limited.

● During the following stage they lose these restrictions, but are still limited to thinking about religious things in concrete terms.

• Only at the final, mature, or fully operational stage of thinking can children think abstractly, think inductively, deduce and hypothesise about religion.

Although Goldman's findings showed that children had to pass from one stage to another, it was also significant that if this was not achieved gradually children ended up with mental blocks about religion which inhibited further development. Put another way, if children were made to run before they could walk, they never learned to run properly. These things were particularly important for the RE of children at the primary stage. Approaches which used metaphor and abstraction were, therefore, inappropriate because children would read into them the literal, concrete imagery of their current stage of thinking and would not grow beyond it. This resulted in the dismissal of religious stories (Bible stories in the 1960s!) which had any symbolic meaning. It also led to a series of concrete experiences in the classroom which were almost totally implicit, or non-religious, because there is scarcely anything in the field of religion which does not have some abstract or symbolic meaning. Many teachers remember this phase since they received their professional training at the time. However, we have had to revise our estimates of Goldman's work.

It is true that we must never try to make children run before they can walk, that we should move from the simple to the abstract, from the general to the detailed, as children's subtlety, sensitivity and comprehension grows. However, this does not mean that the stages which children pass through are tightly related to chronological age.

Goldman did realize this, although he tended to play down the significance of what he had found. He noted that children from 'evangelical sect type' homes tended to have a far better understanding than other children of the same age group. The culturally-rich religious environment that these children experienced clearly had a dramatic effect. This is all the more remarkable because Goldman equated mature religious thinking with a liberal theological approach that would not be found in 'evangelical sect type' homes! But there are other reasons why Goldman's work—although of importance—is limited in value.

First, Goldman probably hitched himself too closely to Piaget's star. It has been shown that Piaget's stages were, to some extent, culturally biased. Ages and stages which apply to Western European children do not appear to apply to children of some other cultures. Worse, Piaget's stages may be the result of a particular form of questioning put to the children. Margaret Donaldson in *Children's Minds* showed that if children were asked the same question, but in a different form, it was often possible for them to reach stages which Piaget believed to be impossible.

Secondly, Goldman probably separated the development of children's thinking from the development of their feelings and so created a conceptual situation which does not exist in real life. It is true that progress and understanding of the development of the human mind has occurred when researchers have isolated elements from each other. But it is also true that results obtained when one part of human behaviour is isolated from another are not necessarily valid for the whole. This is particularly important for the primary stage child. The child's world is not broken up into artificial elements; life is seen as a whole. Until the advent of the National Curriculum for primary schools this was always recognized in the approach to the curriculum, because there is a resistance towards differentiating the field of knowledge into secondary style 'subjects'. 'Subjects' have therefore been integrated, with children studying broad topics. Goldman may have gone too far in restricting religious education to RE; there is an important place for religious education integrated with other subjects.

In normal human development, the intellect does not grow in isolation. Intellect, emotions and social experience grow and develop together. We learn appropriate emotions and appropriate social behaviour. This is why some children of limited mental ability have emotional and social problems; they have not learned to behave appropriately in the social and emotional sphere. It is therefore necessary for emotional development to be considered alongside the development of religious understanding.

It is possible to approach RE entirely through the intellect. But it is also possible to approach RE entirely through the emotions. Bissoner, a Roman Catholic, utilized children's emotions to bring about religious reaction when the intellect was so retarded that the use of understanding was not possible. His approach, which involved surrounding children with love and care, supporting them by prayer, and communicating through basic Christian symbols of light and water to bring them into a relationship with Jesus, is not something that would ever happen in a County School. However, it illustrates how RE can be approached solely through the emotions. Goldman did not realize that the religious development of children was stimulated in homes where there was an emotional dimension to faith.

It is important for teachers to realize that not only will children's development in RE vary tremendously according to their home background, but that, without emotional content, religious understanding will be false. Imagination must be used to help children to begin to feel what it is like to be a believer and sensitivity encouraged to enable children to feel what it is like to be misunderstood or to be mocked for one's faith.

BALANCE IN METHODS OF APPROACH

We are now in a position to look at different methods of approach to Religious Education. Often when we think of primary education we think in terms of topics—maths topics on shapes, topics on the Third World which combine health education, geography and social studies, and topics which combine reading, writing, art and craft. Topics are centres of interest which enable a teacher to bring together skills and related material from different areas of the curriculum or to use different materials and approaches within one area of the curriculum.

In RE, however, we normally refer to themes rather than topics. 'Themes' was adopted as the preferred term when practitioners were struggling to find the right approach to implicit RE. It is a term which has remained with us, being used to indicate that the purpose of the content is entirely religious. A theme is a centre of interest or focus for teaching RE. There are four ways of approaching RE through themes.

Secular themes

These are themes which do not look like Religious Education at all. When one looks at a list of themes such as the life-cycle, peace, light, justice and freedom, right and wrong, it does not immediately spell out 'Religious Education'. There are two kinds of theme here. One kind is involved in implicit RE—providing language and experience crucial for later understanding. The other kind provides the centre from which the objectives of the syllabus can be fulfilled. Let us look at two examples which show both of these approaches to secular themes:

AN IMPLICIT THEME ON LIGHT

Children will learn that without light life is impossible . . .

. . . and will be helped to understand the meaning of 'let there be light' in the creation story in the Bible.

Children will learn that light is in fact made up of many colours, as shown in the rainbow, and may learn the story of Noah and the Rainbow . . .

. . . and will later appreciate that there are some things such as beauty which cannot be measured; that there are hidden things in the world around us.

Children will learn how features of light make it possible to use a magnifying glass . . .

. . . and will be prepared for the ideas of law in the universe—that it is an ordered place.

Children will learn how to make light and use batteries, bulbs and wires to make torches . . .

. . . and will later see why Jesus claimed to be the light of the world as a means of seeing in the darkness, as a revelation.

Children will read stories where light is sometimes used to symbolize good and sometimes to symbolize freedom . . .

. . . and later will understand the symbolism of light in the festivals of Diwali and Hanukkah.

A THEME ON THE LIFE-CYCLE

Birth of animals and babies, the development of a seed and metamorphosis of a butterfly . . .

. . . lead to the feelings of awe and wonder which are part of peak experiences.

Thinking about the family, parents and children, and caring for each other, sharing with each other . . .

. . . leads to understanding of the idea of identity and security.

Naming ceremonies, initiation rites, weddings and funerals . . .

. . . lead to ideas about the passage of life and of development.

Birthdays, weddings and anniversaries . . .

. . . link to religious activities as celebrations.

Discussing questions about reincarnation and resurrection, the overcoming of evil by good, and the power of God . . .

. . . leads to the beginning of understanding of religious ideas.

Dance expressing metamorphosis from chrysalis to butterfly . . .

. . . develops a new area of self-expression.

Religious themes

The second approach is through 'exploring religious themes'. Just as children look at shapes in mathematics, maps in geography, and defence and siege systems in history/technology, there are religious themes which children can follow with interest too. The list is endless, but here are a few suggestions:

    Places of pilgrimage
    Places of worship
    Stories from sacred writings
    Important figures
    Art in religion
    Religious festivals . . .

In looking at places of pilgrimage, children will learn about pilgrimage to Haridwar on the Ganges, the sacred obligation for a Muslim to go to Makka and the importance of the Western Wall in Jerusalem to Jews. They will find that although Christians used to visit places of pilgrimage, like the Beckett shrine in Canterbury and the Alban shrine at St Albans, this became less common after the Reformation and now tends to be confined to places such as Lourdes, Walsingham, and walks along the Via Dolorosa in Jerusalem. This opens up the whole question of what Christians might do instead.

General topics and RE

The third approach concerns religious input into a general topic (not a theme because, as we have already noted, themes are exclusively religious). The commonly followed primary school topic 'exploring our neighbourhood' is a good example. Every curriculum area can be involved.

● In looking at transport, buildings, local events, museums and pillar boxes, history is included.

● In studying old and recent maps, in tracing the origins of food in the shops, in linking the local buses, trains, and telephones to the national communication system, geography is involved.

● In dealing with distances, graphs, shapes, time and distance, mathematics is involved.

● And in looking at the local religious buildings, finding out who goes there, how worship is conducted, how festivals are celebrated, what dress is worn, how the church gets involved in the community, Religious Education is involved.

Although this is the most common topic of this kind, some teachers have successfully involved RE in general topics on travel, leaders, the family, and signs and symbols.

It is likely that the balances of approach will change as the child matures. If there are aspects of religion which cannot be understood until later, then earlier work will tend to emphasize the implicit. This means that there is likely to be a higher level of implicit RE in the infant department than in the juniors; but there will be more implicit RE in the first year of the junior scheme of work than in the fourth year of the junior scheme of work.

Another way of looking at this is to say that at the infant stage there are certain foundation experiences that are necessary for the understanding which will follow. Carol Mumford[2] suggests a number of foundation experiences which have important possibilities for aiding understanding. The first is clearly in a Christian context.

Foundation experience	Possibility of understanding
1. Consistent care in a community; significance in a community leads to:	The Christian teaching that:
feelings of trust and security;	God can be trusted and his love relied on.
realization that care does not stop if we are naughty, and things can be put right;	God still loves us when things go wrong;
awareness of being valued as a person;	God cares for everybody;
appropriate response.	God seeks a free response to love.
2. Children's questions about death.	Human insecurity and mystery of life.
3. Observation of natural processes such as metamorphosis.	Awe in the natural world.
4. Awareness of the changing nature of things (seed/bulb to flower).	Hope and new life.

5. Self-expression.	Relation between inner feeling and outward expression; the idea of symbolism.
6. Experiences which quicken an imagination and lead to use of figurative language. Imaginative identification with story characters.	Religious language and mythology.
7. Exploration experiments with water, light and so on.	Symbolic significance of fire, water, light and so on in religion.
8. Experience of a school community.	The experience of a religious community.
9. Celebration of festivals.	Importance of festivals in religion.
10. Special occasions.	Importance of ritual in religion.

RE and assembly

Although not strictly an 'approach' to RE, we cannot leave this section without looking at possible links between RE and assembly. In one sense, of course, the two are quite distinct and quite different. This is emphasized in Government circulars. The circular on length and control of school sessions says that 5–7–year-olds should have a minimum of 21 hours teaching per week, and 8–13–year-olds a minimum of 23 hours. It goes on to say, 'These hours should include religious education; but not the statutory daily act of collective worship . . .'

RE comes under local regulations in the sense that the syllabus is prescribed by a local conference. Assembly comes under national regulations in that the regulations which apply to all schools are contained in the Education Reform Act. One always has been linked to the classroom and the other to the hall. It would not, therefore, be possible to say that all the required RE is 'done in assembly'. But at the same time there are many important links. Both collective worship and Religious Education come under the heading of Religious Education in the Act and this continues a strong tradition.

Before 1988, 'Religious Instruction and Collective Worship' made up Religious Education. When the 1944 Act came into force it was the intention of legislators to emphasize the cognitive aspects of religion in the classroom and the affective aspects in the hall. Add to this the fact that (as will be explained more fully later) collective worship is always linked to education and not (say) church worship and it is clear that assembly should be linked to Religious Education.

It is, therefore, possible for work which has been done in one class to become a focus for an assembly which involves all classes. It is often a good idea to do this with festivals. Although not recommended for general practice, the scheme has been successfully utilized in some Special Schools where one class per week prepares for an assembly. It normally takes a lot of preparation involving art and craft, writing and research. It is presented before mid-morning break and other classes have their own RE in the session following break, based upon and stimulated by the assembly they have seen.

SUMMING UP ON BALANCES

To summarize the balances we have indicated:

• There must be balance of content which, in effect, means that in a year's RE programme it must be possible to demonstrate how each of the reasons for RE or the RE objectives are being fulfilled. This means that there must be a balance between implicit and explicit RE and a place for developing skills.

● There must be a balance between the RE which will 'happen' because it is part of the everyday life of children in the school and the RE which is planned for by the teacher.

● There must be a balance between the four approaches to RE. The relationship between RE and assembly must not be forgotten.

This immediately raises the question of the allocation of time for RE. The advice I have consistently received from headteachers is that if assemblies are to be carried out properly they will need to constitute about 5 per cent of school time in a week. Similarly, if RE is to be treated properly it will constitute about 5 per cent of curriculum time over a school term. The word 'term' needs underlining. There will be times when RE is central because there is an explicit theme on RE which takes a large amount of time, but there will be times when it does not. Overall the time allocated for Religious Education and for assembly should be about 10 per cent of school time.

The whole thrust of this section has been to encourage balance in the provision of RE. While ensuring balance, there are three other areas which teachers will (as always) need to bear in mind: progression, differentiation and relevance.

It often happens that the RE scheme of work consists of a list of themes/topics to be covered, and it is not always appreciated that there should be a development of learning in which progress and growth is to be seen just as it is in number (maths) and in language. Conscious building up of concepts, enlargement of religious vocabulary, extension of experiences are all involved. So is avoidance of repetition!

While ensuring progression it is also important to remember that most primary classes contain a wide ability range and that teachers need to observe the learning needs of each individual child. Observation of this kind will often lead to the setting up of groups and sub-groups so that activities can be matched to the needs of the particular group. At the same time it must be realized that all children within a sub-group will not have identical needs. Work pitched at the 'average' will fail to stimulate the more able and will cause anxiety to the less able. Work has to be set to allow for different skills and speed of working. To say this is to reiterate what is normal practice in most areas of the curriculum. But unfortunately this does not always happen in RE—although things are likely to improve as teachers become more familiar with the subject-content.

While balance, progression and differentiation are being achieved it is also essential to remember that the work must be relevant to the experiences, needs and interests of the children. It is best to plan themes which relate to the religious experiences of children in the school, whether at home or in the neighbourhood. It is for this reason that the 'six principal world religions' familiar at secondary level are not normally spelled out in the ILEA and other syllabuses for primary schools.

WRITING UP A STATEMENT ON RELIGIOUS EDUCATION

Once the scheme of work is developed within the school it is a legal requirement that parents should be able to know about the curriculum. This arose out of the 'Education (2) Act 1986'. Section 20 says: 'The Secretary of State shall make regulations requiring the governing body of every . . . school to make available to parents of registered pupils at the school . . . such information as to any syllabuses to be followed by those pupils'.

A carefully worded statement about RE should be drawn up so that all concerned parties know what the school's policy is. Experience has shown that the following plan works well.

RELIGIOUS EDUCATION AT . . . SCHOOL

We want to have RE on the curriculum for the following reasons
(Here follow the reasons why the school staff are convinced that

RE is an important part of the curriculum; reasons they would be prepared to stand up for at a parents' meeting. They may not always coincide with reasons for RE given in the Agreed Syllabus, but if there are differences these need to be brought out.)

This is reinforced by law
(This gives an opportunity to explain that RE is part of the basic curriculum that must accord to an Agreed Syllabus and that all children have to undertake it unless withdrawn by parents. It might be advisable to inform parents of special arrangements for withdrawing children.)

The local authority has provided an Agreed Syllabus which says that . . .
(This gives an opportunity to explain what is required for the school in the light of the local Agreed Syllabus and it should also tell parents where they can obtain copies for themselves.)

In this school the Agreed Syllabus will be operated in the following way
(This section will not only set out the scheme of work with the school's statement of aim and the content of the curriculum but it will explain who teaches RE, whether there are teachers with specialist training, whether visits will be made to or from people or places outside the school and what resources are available.)

The school is also required to hold a daily act of collective worship
(Again, the law needs to be explained at this point so that parents are fully able to comprehend the requirements of the law and their own rights.)
   (Much of the material here will be found in the section on assembly.)

In this school the acts of collective worship will be organized in the following way
(It will be necessary to explain the particular approach adopted by the school to provide 'broadly Christian' acts of collective worship and the proportion of such acts, what arrangements are made for withdrawing children and so on.)
(The material needed to write this section of the statement will again be found in the section on assembly.)

EXAMPLES OF GOOD PRACTICE

Having worked through a considerable amount of theory about RE, it would be useful to see RE in practice to assess how far the theory is being carried out and to see a variety of teaching skills in operation. This is made possible by using video. The ILEA, for example, has produced a set of six observational videos and handbooks to enable teachers to see RE in action and to discuss what is going on. The videos are marketed by Pergamon Educational Productions/Religious and Moral Education Press.

These videos plus many other resources including books, artefacts and audio-visual aids are listed in the final section of the book. Another way of considering RE lessons, without having to sit in front of a television screen, is to consider outlines of RE lessons drawn up by a skilled practitioner. Chapter 13 of this book contains model lesson units prepared by Jo Dewar.

REFERENCES

[1] J Cass, *Literature and the Young Child*, Longman
[2] C Mumford, *Young Children and Religion*, Edward Arnold

ACTIVITIES

● Look back at reasons for Religious Education. Which three do you consider to be most important for your school? Give reasons.
● Make a list of things which are likely to happen in your school as starting points for RE and for which you are not likely to have to plan.
● Write a statement on RE for your school.

4
ASSEMBLY—THE ACT OF COLLECTIVE WORSHIP

What should happen in a school assembly[1] is carefully laid down in the law—initially in the 1944 Education Act, and more recently in the 1988 Education Reform Act. The law is set out in two stages.

The legal requirements

1. Since the autumn term of 1988 all schools have had to ensure that children have assembly every day. It is not called 'assembly', but 'collective worship' of which more later. The important thing is that there are three simple rules instead of the five in the 1944 Act.

Under the 1944 Act children had to meet for assembly at the beginning of the day and (unless it was physically impossible because of lack of room, for example) all children had to be in one place. These regulations caused all sorts of problems. Many teachers knew that in their school the assembly was best held mid-morning, before or after break, or at the end of the morning; and it was a good idea to finish Friday afternoon with assembly. But until 1988 this was not allowed.

Another problem was that in a primary school the whole age range from 5–11 had to meet for assembly and teachers were faced with the task of making the assembly relevant to the whole group. In some Special Schools, where ages ranged from 5–16, the problems were even greater. So, in general, there was a big sigh of relief when, in 1988, teachers realized that the two most difficult restrictions had been lifted.

2. From the autumn term of 1989 (1990 in Inner London) County Schools have had to respond to the following changes in the law. The law now states that most acts of collective worship in any school term[2] must be wholly or mainly of a broadly Christian character.[3] According to the wording of the Act this means that they must reflect the broad traditions of Christian belief.[4] However, according to the circular which was published after the Act to clarify matters, not all the material in such an assembly need be Christian.[5] In addition to this, collective worship may occasionally take place off the school premises but only if the school is Voluntary Aided or Grant Maintained.[6] In a County School this would have to be in addition to the normal assembly.

It must be noted that these arrangements do not apply to nursery or to Special Schools. The religious clauses of the Act do not apply to children until they reach statutory school age. Different arrangements are made for Special Schools in that headteachers are expected to do what they can in view of the disadvantage which many children in their schools have to overcome. This is no licence to dispense with assembly altogether, as Schedule 1(9) of the Act says 'provision shall be made in the Regulations to secure that, so far as practicable, every pupil attending a Special School will attend religious worship and receive religious education . . .'

THE CURRENT REQUIREMENTS IN DETAIL

The requirements of the law have caused quite a lot of anxiety and over-reaction. Initially about half the teachers in primary and Special Schools in Inner London were of a mind to use the 'conscience clause' and opt out of assembly. They believed that it was not right to have most assemblies of a Christian kind. The same reaction came from Muslim parents, who used the 'conscience clause' to request that their children should not take part in assemblies predominantly Christian in character. Both reactions were based on a misunderstanding of what the Act actually said!

What does it say then? In law (as distinct from ordinary speech) the words 'mostly' or 'mainly' mean 'at least 51 per cent'. Put in a negative way, this means that about half of the assemblies in a school need not fall into the 'Christian' category. But frankly, for some teachers, some parents and in some situations 49 per cent of assemblies that are non-Christian would not be sufficient. Suppose, for instance, there was a school in which 85 per cent of pupils were Muslim. In such a case many people would feel that it was wrong to force them to attend assemblies half of which were Christian in character. This kind of situation was recognized by those who framed the law and they devised a way of adapting the proportion of Christian to non-Christian assemblies.[7]

If a headteacher, with support of the governors,[8] believed that he/she had a case for changing the ratio (which might, if governors wished, include evidence of parental support from a referendum)[9] they could ask the local Standing Advisory Council for Religious Education (SACRE) for authorization to do so. The way in which such requests should be made to, and how they will be considered by, SACRE will be decided by each SACRE in due course.

WHAT IS THE STANDING ADVISORY COUNCIL FOR RELIGIOUS EDUCATION?

Under the 1944 Education Act, LEAs could, if they wished, set up a SACRE to advise them on Religious Education—'methods of teaching, the choice of books and provision of lectures for teachers'. From 1988 the option was removed and LEAs *had* to set them up.

SACRE is an Advisory Council to advise the LEA about religious worship and RE in County Schools according to the Agreed Syllabus; upon methods of teaching, choice of materials and the provision of training for teachers. SACRE consists of four separate committees: teachers, LEA representatives (who may be elected members, or officers, administrators or inspectors, or both), representatives of the Church of England and representatives of other faiths.[10] Among its new functions, SACRE has to decide whether, bearing in mind the home background of pupils, there is a case for changing the proportion of assemblies in particular schools. Since SACRE works on a 'one committee, one vote' basis, it is necessary for the governors to persuade at least three of the committees. Any decision to vary the proportion of assemblies lasts for five years from a date determined by SACRE itself, but it is open to review at the request of the headteacher and governors during that time.[11]

Despite the variation of the proportion of Christian to non-Christian assemblies some parents may still wish to withdraw their children from the remaining Christian assemblies.[12] Let us suppose that this happens in the case of Muslim children. The headteacher might feel that it would be a good idea for them to have a Muslim assembly which is 'wholly or mainly of a broadly Muslim character', perhaps having an Imam to take the assembly. Such an assembly can be distinctive of a faith, but not of a denomination within a faith. The head cannot decide this alone. Separate assemblies can be organized only for teaching groups (such as infant or junior departments, or separate classes) and not for any religious group.[13] But, again, SACRE can give the authorization to do this if a case is made out in a similar way. Such arrangements do not, in fact, prevent parents from withdrawing their children from these special assemblies.

Before a decision is made to hold separate assemblies the head may wish to consider two alternatives. These alternatives are important as there are very good reasons why all children in a school should be brought together for assembly. The children need to recognize themselves as a group, to learn how to behave in a group and how to 'perform' in front of a group. They need to recognize the structure of the school as it is expressed in the group (especially valuable if non-teaching staff attend). Children need to see how their group relates to the wider community outside the school. They need to understand 'a sense of occasion' and during such a time have the opportunity to reflect and assess. Children who are separated from such school gatherings lose a valuable part of their education.

1. Since 1944 it has been possible for children withdrawn from assembly to be instructed in their own faith off the school premises

at the beginning or the end of the school day. This has been done with the proviso that it did not disrupt the child's education (because for instance they might be late for school or it might encourage absenteeism). In secondary schools it was actually possible for instruction to take place on the school premises provided that no expense fell upon the LEA (theoretically rent of room, light and heat, but in fact the cost of someone to give the instruction). Children in boarding schools could, in addition, worship outside of school on any day of religious observance. This has been continued in the new Act.[14]

2. It has always been possible for a headteacher to support and encourage voluntary extra-curricula activities. Scripture Union groups, Christian Unions and Christian Education Movement groups have been a tradition in some schools. Muslim clubs and societies and provision for midday prayers are becoming more common in other schools.

WHAT CAN WE DO IN ASSEMBLIES?

In the case of County Schools details are worked out by the headteacher after consulting the governing body. In the flexible arrangements allowed for Voluntary Schools details are worked out by the governors in consultation with the headteacher.

The first thing to note is that the assembly must be for Religious Education, not Personal and social Education, not Moral Education nor anything else. This has always been the case. In the 1944 Act the Religious Instruction (which went on in the classroom) and the 'collective worship' (which went on in assembly) together constituted Religious Education. The new Education Reform Act has tried to update the language because RI had given way to Religious Studies (RS) or Religious Education (RE). The law has been reduced to saying that Religious Education (which takes place in the classroom) and the 'collective worship' together constitute Religious Education. There is no getting away from the fact.

But it is important to emphasize that what happens in 'collective worship'—or assembly—is not the same as what happens in the church down the road, or in any other place where believers meet

70

for worship. This is so seldom understood that it needs spelling out.

● What happens in the assembly is educational. Something that happens in a church service might be educational—it depends on the quality of the sermon! But there are many things which are not educational. In a Christian context the Eucharist or Holy Communion is not educational but sacramental: the joining together in prayer is not educational but devotional. In a school the assembly is always part of a child's education. This is not to say that children will not see the demonstration of a sacrament or listen to a prayer, but the purpose is educational.

● What happens in the assembly is 'collective worship' and not 'corporate worship'. Corporate worship is possible only for a body (corpus) of believers. It was recognized, even in 1944, that when a large proportion of children in school are adherents of Christian churches of different denominations they do not constitute a body. The appropriate worship is that which fits a collection of individuals. Interestingly, when the 1944 Education Act was first drafted the term 'corporate' was used, but it was altered for the final writing. This fact is reinforced by the insistence within the Act that the assembly should be non-denominational. Except in inter-church/inter-faith gatherings worship is always denominational.

So what *can* be done in an assembly? Worship itself is a contraction of an anglo-saxon term, 'worthship', used to describe that which was of highest or greatest worth. The citizen of greatest worth is 'his or her worship the mayor'. When people are in love, each 'worships the very ground' the other walks upon. Obviously, to Christians, God is the object of highest worth, but this would not be true for everyone. In the context of Religious Education, collective worship is therefore the celebration of that which is of highest worth to the school community.[15]

NON-CHRISTIAN ASSEMBLIES

There are many ways of celebrating things of worth and importance to the school community within the context of Religious Education.

71

Here are six *possibilities*; not the only types of non-Christian assembly.

Multi-faith assemblies

The assembly should focus on an issue to which all faiths represented in the school can contribute. This will be a religious assembly, but not a Christian-religious assembly. However, it has to be said that the distinction is not at all clear, because it would not be possible to *exclude* Christianity from such an assembly.[16]

All people with a religious faith have things in common which they care about. In general, we can say that all religious people care for the world and for other people—although this is not the exclusive preserve of religious people. A theme of this type provides an opportunity for children in school to see the way that different religions approach the issues through their scriptures, in examples of people who have taken the issue seriously, in their prayers and in their hymns.

Children therefore become conscious of the things religions have in common (caring attitudes, scriptures, prayers) even though they are very different from each other. In fact it is important to emphasize the distinctiveness and the difference, because in this type of assembly children must not go away with the idea that all religions are part of the one. Syncretism of religions devalues each religion by reducing it to the lowest common denominator. In such an assembly it will be possible to tell some of the stories about how the world came into existence. It will be possible to read relevant scriptures. The following comes from Sura xxv.27–28 in the Holy Qur'an:

'Seest thou not that God sends down rain from the sky? With it we can then bring out produce of various colours. And in the mountains are tracts white and red, of various shades of colour and black intense in hue. And so amongst men and crawling creatures and cattle are they of various colours. Those truly fear God among his servants, who have knowledge, for God is exalted in might oft forgiving.'

The point is being made that in nature there are wonderful colours of vegetation, rocks and animal life, and it makes us wonder at God. But those who truly respect God can see wonderful things in the spiritual world as well.

It will be possible to tell other stories. In the Midrash, a collection of teachings and stories which illustrate the Talmud (the Jewish Law), it says:

'A wise Rabbi was walking along a road when he saw a man planting a tree. The Rabbi asked him "How many years will it take for this tree to bear fruit?" The man answered that it would take seventy years. The Rabbi asked "Are you so fit and strong that you expect to live that long and eat its fruit?" The man answered "I found a fruitful world because my forefathers planted for me. So I will do the same for my children."' [17]

Festival assemblies

All religions have special days and festivals. Some, like the Jewish Shabbat, occur weekly but most occur annually. Some festivals bring to mind important stories from the life of the founder of the faith. Buddhists (of the Theravada group) celebrate the birth, enlightenment and death of the Buddha at Wesak. And towards the end of the fast of Ramadan, Muslims remember the start of the revelation of the Qur'an during the Night of Power—Lailat-ul-Quadr.

Other festivals commemorate important happenings: Jews celebrate Purim in memory of deliverance from a Persian enemy in Queen Esther's time about 2,300 years ago. Some festivals commemorate the passing of the year. Holi is a Hindu spring festival and Sukkot is the Jewish harvest festival when the forty years' wilderness wandering at the time of Moses is remembered too. Some festivals centre on theological beliefs. Chinese Buddhists have a festival to help the spirits of the departed who have no place to rest and no descendants to dwell in. Large paper boats are made and offered to spirits in temples. They are then burned to help the spirits to reach peace and rest.

Festivals often commemorate important events in the lives of followers of a particular faith. St Patrick's Day is remembered by some Christians on 17 March.

Imaginative use of festivals can help children to enjoy and to appreciate stories, events and beliefs important to members of particular faiths. But is this worship? It is not the 'corporate worship' which is the norm for believers (in a place set aside for such worship); but the enjoyment and entering in is the 'collective worship' required of an assembly.

There are, however, problems for those arranging assemblies.

● Most teachers are unaware of the wealth of festivals or when they occur. This is easy to remedy. Every year the 'Shap Calendar of Religious Festivals' is published by the Commission for Racial Equality,[18] for the Shap Working Party on World Religions. There are a number of books which help too. Martin Palmer's *Faiths and Festivals*[19] summarizes the stories and events of twenty-three festivals and also looks at festivals associated with the significant events in life (birth, maturity, marriage, death) in different religions. The Religious and Moral Education Press publish a series of books in their *Living Festival* Series[20] that have much more detail. Where there are children of these faiths in school and parents supporting them, their advice and help can be invaluable at such a time. It is also possible to use certain service books associated with festivals. The Board of Deputies of British Jews publish a simplified text for the Passover meal together with notes about the Seder, called *The Seder Handbook*.[21]

● It is clear, looking at the resources, that it would be easy for assemblies to be swamped with festivals. They cannot be dealt with fully in only one assembly for each, but to deal with a few might be unfair, and to deal with them all would be unbalanced. Clearly a selection has to be made, on the basis of relevance to the children in the school and relevance for the local community. If this means that there are too few (for example in areas where there is a uniform Christian culture), additional festivals should be selected for their importance. Martin Palmer's book and the *Living Festival* Series are good guides. But even so, we are left with about twenty festivals and many other themes to cover in assemblies. The solution is to deal with each festival, in depth, twice—once during a child's movement through the infant department and once during the junior years. The assembly dealing with the festival need then take place only on the day concerned, referring back, or forwards, to the classroom experience.

● There is a problem about how far children should learn by participation. Most parents find it acceptable for their children to learn about a festival celebrated by children of another faith, providing that it is children of that faith who are doing the celebrating. Parents may, however, have serious reservations about their own children actually participating in the celebration, fearing this might tacitly turn children into believers. All the evidence suggests that this does not, in fact, happen because children know that they are in a 'let's pretend' situation, just as in any other kind of role play. Indeed, the assumption some teachers make that children learn through imaginative experience seems to me to be just wishful thinking. There is no guarantee that the feelings that children experience in role play are the same as those of a real believer. It all depends whether the imaginative experience is correct and authentic!

Nevertheless participation does worry some parents. Some Muslim parents, for example, believe that if their child were to take part in an assembly based on Christian worship it would involve them in sin. Ghulam Sarwar, the Director of the Muslim Educational Trust in *What can Muslims Do?* (responding to the Education Reform Act) says that when Muslim children 'pray to Jesus as "Son of God", learn about the "Trinity" and thus commit the awesome sin of Shirk associating others with Allah this is the worst thing a Muslim can do'.

Some Christian parents who are aware of the dangers of the spirit world and wish to leave it well alone, believe that spirits might well be involved in, for example, Hindu worship and that their children could be brought into potentially harmful contact with that world.[22]

For both groups there is a line to be drawn—which is often quite difficult to define—beyond which parents will not go. Some parents do have a tender conscience and just as, in Christian terms, Paul was prepared to regulate his own Christian life to meet the needs of tender Christian conscience in Corinth (1 Corinthians chapter 8, New Testament), so the school needs to be prepared to allow for parents wishing their children to opt out of such levels of participation.

● There is another problem which relates to participation by believing children. Teachers should never assume that all children of one faith celebrate a festival in the same way. There are regional and even theological variations in all religions. If, upon enquiry, differences are revealed it is best to draw them out and explain them. However, teachers should not assume that everything children tell them about a festival is reliable! Parents are much more reliable and consulting one of the local leaders of the religious community would be even better. Indeed it is generally best to consult local religious leaders because in some faiths there would be concern if children were to be involved in teaching about the festival. Religious leaders will normally be delighted to be consulted and keen to help.

Story assemblies

Stories have always been one of the key ways to transmit religious thought and practice; and young children love stories. Story is therefore an essential focus for assembly.

Before the Jewish Taanach (the Christian's 'Old Testament') was written down, it was probably recited round the camp fires at night and the stories were accurately passed from generation to generation. All of the great religious leaders have been story-tellers, putting their teaching into words which grip the hearts and minds of listeners, making their teaching easily memorable. Some stories tell of the lives of founders and followers, some give the essence of their teaching, some indicate the reason for moral behaviour—all presented in a way which is instantly understood.

Many teachers have denied that young children are able to understand higher theological concepts. Recent research, however, has demonstrated that it is not the concepts which are unattainable, but the way they are presented by the teacher which puts the concepts beyond the reach of the child. Many ideas which Piaget 'proved' could not be understood by young children have been shown by Margaret Donaldson to be perfectly understandable if children are approached in the right way.[23] To take a Christian example: the ideas involved in the Christian belief that God himself came into the world in the person of Jesus Christ to bring together his love (in forgiveness of sin) and his justice (in punishment of sin) in the one act of the crucifixion are deemed to be beyond little children. But consider now the following story which comes from an Islamic cultural background.

'A Persian Caliph once agreed with his counsellors that he should increase his powers by increasing the number of laws which people had to obey or else they would receive 30 stripes. At the next meeting of the Council, it was revealed that the Caliph's mother had broken all of the new laws. The Caliph was in a dilemma. If he condemned his mother to 30 lashes she would die and because it would prove him to be a man without love he would lose his kingdom. But if he forgave his mother it would prove him to be a ruler without justice and he would lose his kingdom for that too. So he convened the court, had his mother charged and when it was proved that she was guilty passed the full sentence of 30 lashes. Then he left his throne and went to his mother. He took her and set her on his throne and returned and stood in her place. He bared his own back and received the 30 lashes proving that he was a ruler of love and a ruler of justice at the same time and his kingdom was saved.'

At one level this is a good story; at another a good example of a clever man and a wise ruler; at another still unrealized level, a way of understanding an aspect of Christian theology.

Another unforgettable story from Islamic culture tells how a man had a dream and in the dream came to two identical doors in a wall. One was marked 'happiness' and the other 'unhappiness'. Entering the door marked 'unhappiness' he found himself in a large room. At its centre was a large, round table bearing everything good to eat.

77

Guests were seated round the table. But the left arm of each guest was tied to his or her left side, and each person's right arm was tied to a long-handled wooden spoon which acted like a splint so that they could not bend their elbows. They could reach the food with their spoons, but could not get it to their mouths so they were unhappy. Leaving the room to go next door he was surprised to find that everything was identical except that all of the guests were happy. In the 'happiness' room each guest was using his spoon to feed his neighbour on the right.

The story is so simple, it is moral, it is unforgettable. Every religious culture has scores of such stories.[24]

Demonstration assemblies

Assemblies which focus on religious festivals give children insight into religious beliefs and practices. But there are many more aspects of religion which are taught through symbolism.

Ritual in its many forms is a way of bringing a particular group of believers together in what, for them, is a real act of worship, while for others it offers insight into what a real act of worship is like. I have sat with non-Muslim children on a number of occasions when children of Muslim faith have explained Salah (prayer) to them, giving them an understanding of the meaning of the actions and of the words which are used. As the explanation culminates in the act of worship it is at once a real act of worship and a valuable act of observation and education.

Such assemblies can be extended beyond the children to include members of the community, invited into school to explain some aspect of their faith or practice. The important thing to remember is that any member of the community coming into school will need to be very carefully briefed (in writing) on what to expect and what is expected of them. They should be given a time limit and reminded that the purpose of the visit is to explain part of their faith and practice and not to attempt to persuade, evangelize, convert or proselytize in any way. In many respects it is best for the speaker to be used by the teacher in exactly the same way as the teacher would use any other resource.

'Peak experience' assemblies

Peak experiences are special and occasional: peak experience assemblies are special and occasional too, and they need more preparation than most other types of assembly.

A 'peak experience' is an experience which 'turns people on to religion'. It is important that children have such experiences because they provide the opportunity for personal, in depth, self-examination in a way which is often the start of a new movement towards maturity. It is also important that children have such experiences because it helps them to understand why some of their friends are 'religious'.

One aspect of some assemblies is the awakening of awe and wonder in children, often achieved through natural beauty. During a weekend a school had been used to host a flower show. As children filed into the hall on Monday morning, the very best of the flower display exhibits was in a central place on the stage. The stage itself has been blacked out by curtaining and the display was spotlighted. As the playing of the Pastoral Symphony quietened, concentration was fixed upon the flowers and their arrangement. There was a time of quietness. Nothing was said. And then the children quietly left the hall. Some children have never forgotten that moment because it was different, even 'crazy'. But others have remembered it because they saw the partnership between God and humanity which is creative and beautiful.

But peak experiences go beyond awe and wonder. Many people become religious when they find a religious answer to the fundamental questions of existence which we all face—'Who am I?' 'Why am I here?' 'What is the meaning of life?' 'What is Death?' Assemblies which help children to recognize the existence of such questions, help them to understand the answers which have been given, and encourage them to find answers for themselves, are crucial. The reason why adults often crack up under pressure is because they do not have personal answers to these questions. Life seems to be pointless when one cannot say with assurance that 'I know why I am here'.

It goes beyond this. Children face crises over these very problems. In one Inner London school birds nested in a corner of a quiet inner courtyard. The teacher in the junior department responsible for science rigged up a system of mirrors and lenses so that children could observe the magic of laying, hatching and feeding. The day came when the nestlings would fly, but the structure of the inner walls was such that they flew into them and died. It was a crisis for many children who had lived through the cycle from birth to death so quickly. The crisis was met by a sensitive headteacher who devised an assembly to enable them cope and come to terms with what happened.

This illustrates another point. Assemblies have to be planned. In the primary school it is best for the school staff to have 'assembly' on the agenda for staff meetings and to plan a balanced programme of assemblies for half a term in advance, so that it is possible to seek the help of parents, arrange a visiting participant and capitalize on festivals which are coming by linking the assembly to craft work in the classroom. But the programme should never be inflexible. A need or an opportunity for a special assembly should always take priority over a normal programme.

Spiritual development assemblies

Spirituality assemblies are designed to foster the growth of the human spirit. It is important to emphasize this meaning because there are two quite different meanings of the word 'spiritual' which are used in Religious Education.

One way of understanding 'spiritual' relates to the development of the inner life in relation to God. When we use what can be seen about a religion to achieve an understanding of the unseen elements which lie behind it we are using the word in a religious way.

But the word 'spiritual' can also be used in a non-religious way with reference to the growth of the human spirit or human personality. Sometimes these meanings are used interchangeably, even contradictorily, without the user being aware of the significance. HMI writing in *The Curriculum from 5 to 16*[25] seem to see one aspect of spirituality in general terms and another in narrower terms: '(The Spiritual) area of learning and experience points at its most general to feelings and convictions about the significance of human life and the world as a whole . . . Religious Education . . . is contained within this but is not identical with it.'

James Fowler believed that the human spirit grows in stages. In his book *Stages of Faith*[26] he identifies stages which most of us would recognize.

● There is a stage which he calls *intuitive-projective faith* where the person imitates adults and is strongly influenced by adult example, mood, action and stories from his/her own community. At this stage there is a strong emphasis on intuition and feelings. Most teachers would identify this stage with the infant stage—although Fowler would not say this.

● The next stage he identified as the *mythic-literal stage* when the person takes on beliefs, stories and standard observances for him or herself: at this stage story is more important than intuition and feelings. Fowler was able to show that a person moves from one stage to another as a result of the desire to know what things really are so that the distinction can be made between the real and the imaginary.

● Fowler identified a further stage which he called *synthetic-conventional faith*. This is where a person relates the views she/he holds with the views of friends and others who are important to them so that a synthesis takes place. This is clearly made possible as the person becomes aware of other views, of clashes and contradictions in stories and begins to look for meaning rather than literal truth. Again many people would see the second and third stages as marking the beginning and end of junior school experience, but in fact the development is not age related but experience related.

● A fourth stage is relevant to us here. Fowler called it *individuative-reflective faith* where the consensus views previously held are evaluated critically and personal views are held, not because of others but because of personal critical reflection. The self becomes independent of others and accepts its own world view. This arises when a person becomes conscious of differences of viewpoint among contemporaries; differences that mean consensus becomes impossible. Fowler went on to observe that some people never reach this or some of the other stages.

If Fowler's analysis is correct, assemblies can be used to provide growth points that enable a child to move from one stage to another—helping children to distinguish between the real and the imaginary, challenging the views held by pupils with the views of others, leading children into the process of evaluating and revaluating their own position. Indeed in some respects this might be said to be inherent in all of the earlier assemblies: but here the purpose becomes explicit rather than implicit.

Let us not lose our way; we have now looked at six examples of the kind of assembly which can be provided in the 49 per cent of assembly time designated as non-Christian. In fact it will quickly be apparent that a strict 51 per cent:49 per cent split is not possible. Christianity has to be involved in a multi-faith assembly. Is an assembly of this type Christian or non-Christian? Who knows? Christianity could not be excluded from some of the peak experience assemblies either. The 50:50 division is, therefore, a rough guide, not a task master but a reminder to headteachers that a balance needs to be kept.

CHRISTIAN ASSEMBLIES

Many people express a fear of Christian assemblies because they feel they go back to a position where assemblies were conducted as real acts of worship reaching children through emotion rather than through their rationality. Indeed, as I mentioned earlier, there was a time when it was said that 'what is taught in the classroom is caught in the assembly'. It is important to realize that those days are gone. They were never required by the law, and they are prohibited by law now.

So what can we do in Christian assemblies? It is as well to remind ourselves of the actual words of the Act. The Act says that such assemblies must be 'wholly or mainly of a broadly Christian character' and goes on to say that this means they should reflect the 'broad traditions of Christian belief'.

First we must note that this definition is extremely wide. The forms of worship practised by Orthodox, Roman Catholic, Reformed, Anglican, Free Churches, Pentecostals, Brethren, Quakers . . . are very diverse. They range from noise to silence, ritual to complete freedom, movement to stillness, elaborate surroundings to plain ones. But the Act does specify Christian beliefs.

Christians have different kinds of beliefs—doctrinal beliefs, beliefs about how to worship and moral beliefs. Again the range is pretty wide. In fact, so wide that it is clear that in some cases exactly the same form of assembly provided in the 'non-Christian' terms of reference can be provided within the 'Christian' terms of reference. Indeed the multi-faith assembly might sometimes, and by some people, be recognized as a Christian assembly. It depends upon semantics! Let us start then with four focal points:

Focus on beliefs which Christians share with others.
Christians have beliefs which they share with all other religious believers and with other men and women of good will. These areas can become a focus for the assembly. In this respect the 'Charities' series published by the Religious and Moral Education Press might be found very useful. These books deal with Christian Aid, Help the Aged, the Samaritans, Shelter, and so on. Many of the charities have a Christian foundation but the area of concern is one shared with people of other faiths too.

Focus on Christian beliefs expressed in festivals.

Focus on Christian beliefs expressed in story.

Focus on Christian beliefs expressed in ritual.

It will be seen at once that these last three types of assembly are exactly like the three types of non-Christian assemblies mentioned earlier. Three things need to be noticed:

● There are only two major Christian festivals—Christmas and Easter—in Christian belief which focus on the entry of God into this world in the person of Jesus, and on the departure of God from this world in the person of Jesus at the time of his death, resurrection and ascension. (Some Christians specifically keep Ascension Day apart.)

These occasions are especially suitable for actual acts of Christian worship for Christians in the school. Whitsun celebrates the birthday of the church in the arrival of the Holy Spirit to dwell in every Christian but it is extremely difficult to communicate this to children. Indeed it is very difficult for anyone other than a Christian who knows from personal experience how the Holy Spirit operates in his/her life to explain this at all.

This raises an important point: it is often assumed that it needs a believer to teach about a faith. This is not true. It takes a committed teacher to teach about a faith—a teacher who has the commitment to read, research, ask, visit, prepare and so on. The truth is that the teacher is limited to the seen and the rational. It is very easy for a teacher to describe the structure and meaning of the architecture of a Gurdwarah; the teacher can accurately describe what is required of a Muslim in acts of devotion; the teacher can tell a story which has been used for centuries to transmit a faith. But the teacher cannot, unless he is a Jew, actually know what it feels like to be a Jewish boy at his Bar Mitzvah; and she cannot, unless she is a Christian, baptized in the Spirit, know what happens and what gives rise to praising God with the gift of tongues. It is at this point that teachers must accept their limitations and use the experience of people as resources.

To return to Christian festivals—saints' days are important for many Christians and are set aside so that the saints can be remembered. A complete calendar and saints' stories in outline is given in Attwater's *Penguin Dictionary of Saints*.

All Saints Day, on 1 November, is used to remember all the unremembered saints of the church. This is preferable to any remembrance on All Hallows Eve (Hallowe'en) on the last day of October—indeed this festival is best avoided altogether. Hallowe'en can cause disturbance (sometimes serious), through fear, to children; it certainly gives the wrong view of many innocent women who were put to death as witches in Medieval Britain. Hallowe'en is also offensive to members of the Christian and Jewish faiths who

ASSEMBLY—THE ACT OF COLLECTIVE WORSHIP

believe in the reality of the (evil) spirit world. Problems arising from Hallowe'en celebrations are regularly catalogued in publications of the Evangelical Alliance.

● The best book of Bible stories I have found is Pat Alexander's *The Lion Children's Bible* (Lion Publishing). This hardback edition is exactly the same as *The Puffin Children's Bible* in paperback. Another useful series of stories is the *Faith in Action* series published by the Religious and Moral Education Press. This series includes up-to-date stories of the work of Brother Andrew, Jackie Pullinger, Cicely Saunders, Corrie Ten Boom and many more. A list of back-up resources in each of the books makes them useful for assembly.

● For cultural reasons, Christian ritual is an area that many parents—even those who make no profession of Christian faith themselves—expect to be included in assembly. Quite apart from those areas of Christian ritual which might form a focus for assembly—the demonstration of a doll being baptized, showing the changes in colour of clergy robes through the year, listening to a local Christian rock band playing modern Christian music—there are a number of things which most parents want their children to know about.

Many parents expect assembly themes to include the Lord's Prayer, the Ten Commandments, the 23rd Psalm, sometimes the Beatitudes and (declared at one public meeting just after Cup Final day) 'Abide with Me'. There is no reason why some assemblies should not focus upon such themes so that children understand where the rituals came from, what they mean, how Christians use them and so on.

However, many teachers voice concern about whether children should say the Lord's Prayer . . . the Ten Commandments . . . and so on. They argue that children should only 'say' prayers if they are involved as believers.

If I take assembly in a mixed-faith/non-faith situation and I want to draw to a conclusion I sometimes suggest a 'thinking time', a quietness to let what has been said sink in or 'speak' to the children. It is a good educational, as well as Quaker, strategy. But sometimes I will say, 'I am a Christian and because I am Christian I often pray to God as if he was a father to me. Those of you who are Christians can join in with me in your thoughts if you wish and say "Amen" at the end. Those of you who are not Christians should simply watch and listen and you will begin to understand one way in which a Christian prays.'

Threshold worship. Christian worship is a highly complex activity with many parts to it. Some Christians believe that children can worship, although they would describe it as worship 'in a simple way'. If we define worship as 'worth-ship', as we did earlier, then this belief seems reasonable. In Christian worship a child acts so as to give Jesus a place of highest worth. But those who believe that worship is highly complex would dismiss this activity, saying that it cannot be compared with true worship. Some would go further and dismiss the child's activity as 'threshold worship'. As the term is now used it focuses upon two different forms of assembly.

Implicit worship

We used the word 'implicit' earlier to describe something 'hidden inside' something else. But when we use the word 'implicit' in Religious Education we normally use it in a different, highly technical and specific way.

Implicit RE gives children language and experience at an ordinary, normally non-religious, level so that they will be able to enter into and understand religious language and experience at a later stage. Implicit RE provides this non-religious experience. If children are to understand the awe and wonder involved in worship they need to have experienced awe and wonder at the nature table, for example, so that they relate the two experiences. If children are to understand the nature of God's forgiveness in the Christian faith, they need to have experienced the suffering of the innocent for the guilty and to know that once punishment has been given there is nothing more to pay.

So in the area of worship it is necessary for children to experience and verbalize things at a lower level, so that one day they will be able to understand at a higher level. This is 'implicit (or threshold) worship'.

Think for a moment of what might be involved in worship: music, singing, prayer, meditation, silence, exaltation, fellowship, praise. In the primary school children might well be able to cope with the first six in our list, but it is much less likely they will understand what fellowship and praise mean in the context of worship. An assembly that focuses on the school community—its mutual concerns, hopes and expectations—may not seem like worship but it is a step towards the experience of fellowship that is at the heart of worship. An assembly that focuses upon praise for work well done, tasks successfully achieved, and service to others faithfully rendered, may not seem like worship, but it is a prerequisite for the full understanding of praise. An assembly featuring the return of a school party from the ski slopes that evokes feelings of 'We are glad you had such a good time', 'Well done for getting your certificates', 'We are sorry for the boy who broke his leg', and 'We are looking forward to going next year' (school visits legislation permitting!) is a crucial step in preparing children for the understanding of worship.

Restricted worship

Look again at the list of elements of Christian worship itemized above (many of which are common to other faiths too), and add others which come to mind. These could include submission, dedication, atonement, affirmation, celebration, concern, sense of smallness in the presence of something greater, stillness, restoration. No child (perhaps no adult!) can bring all of these elements into a whole. So why not focus upon just one of the elements of worship? As soon as we do this we are back in threshold worship, because mere silence, exaltation, fellowship would not be described as worship—but it is in the sense that we now understand 'implicit worship'. The danger with such forms of worship in assembly is that some headteachers might be tempted to use implicit forms of assembly almost entirely because they fit with what has been done in the past and because they feel more at home with this form of assembly. It is therefore important to note that this is only one approach (out of twelve) to assembly and anybody who makes it their business to check on assembly will expect to see a proper balance across all assembly types; not simply a 50:50 split between Christian and non-Christian.

WHERE DOES THIS LEAVE
THE HEADTEACHER?

The headteacher is involved in many aspects of the assembly. The head is required to ensure that the legal provisions for assembly are met and will have to be able to demonstrate that they are being met. There is a simple way to do this.

If a staff meeting or an assembly committee draws up an assembly plan or forecast by the half term, then the plan only needs initialling on a daily basis to confirm that what was planned has been done. This task will not be difficult for an assembly committee or a staff room agenda if plans are made on the basis of a 'theme a week'; indeed, finding interesting weekly titles that can be featured on the school noticeboard or displayed on one side of the hall stage can be a stimulating task.

If the week's theme is introduced on the Monday by the head and concluded on the Friday by the deputy, the three remaining days can be set aside for a class-led assembly, or for the class teacher, for a visitor or for music.

When the planning is being done it needs to be remembered that the law now permits flexible groupings, provided that the groups are teaching groups. It is therefore possible to hold separate infant and junior assemblies. In a large school, year assemblies might sometimes be valuable and class assemblies are always a possibility. Do not forget that words are only one form of communication. Communication takes place through music, mime, art, drama and dance, although care must be taken not to offend children or parents for whom dance and drama is suspect, as it is for many Muslims.

It is important to remember to use all the expertise which is available. Occasionally (very occasionally in primary schools!) there will be a member of staff who has received professional training for contemporary RE. Sometimes there will be members of staff who have a particular religious faith who will be willing to check the accuracy of the information given in an assembly and might even be persuaded to help directly. Assembly books do not always provide the expertise and it is better to use the living resources within a school rather than books of assemblies.

Nevertheless there are a large number of assembly books published and in use. It is best to assess these books by using the following criteria.

Do the books provide material from a number of faiths? Do they provide authentic stories? Do they follow equal opportunities policies? Are they at the right level for the children? Do they deal with the important and not the trivial?

The headteacher's responsibilities do not end here. Head-teachers have responsibilities to themselves. The head may feel that, in all conscience, she/he cannot lead an assembly which is part of Religious Education. The new Act has made it quite clear that the head may opt out of taking assembly in exactly the same way as a teacher has always been able to do so. But having said this, the head is still responsible for seeing that the assemblies take place. There is an element of the stick as well as the carrot in the Education Reform Act. Headteachers and governors of large schools will find themselves responsible for the financial management of their schools. If the head has to employ external help to provide for assemblies (and of course RE too) that help has to be paid for and there will be less money available for other vital things.

Suppose there is a complaint (these most frequently come from governors, but sometimes from parents) that the assemblies in the school are not being conducted in the way required under the Education Act. Until the 1988 Education Reform Act such complaints went to the Secretary of State and a letter would be received by the LEA concerned requesting that assurance be given that the school in question is keeping to every part of the law. If the Authority did not give, or could not give, that assurance, the Secretary of State commenced proceedings to bring the Authority before a court for default. In fact no such case ever reached the courts because things were always put right in schools before the matter got that far.

Under the new Act complaints will no longer be made to the Secretary of State unless the person making the complaint claims that the LEA has not done its duty in dealing with a complaint itself. Every LEA has to set up a complaints procedure to deal with complaints made about RE, assembly and the National Curriculum so that complaints can be dealt with satisfactorily. So far as RE and assembly are concerned the Authority can ask the Standing Advisory Council for Religious Education (SACRE) to deal with such matters on its behalf; but it does not have to do so. Ultimately the LEA and governors have joint responsibility for seeing that the law is carried out (Section 10[1]).

There is, however, another fundamental difference between the situation before and after the new Education Act. Under the old arrangements the complainant was never known to the school or the LEA because the letter from the Department of Education and Science gave the complainant anonymity. Under the new arrangements the LEA will know who has made the complaint. This could discourage people from making a complaint if, for example, it affected relationships with other governors or even a child's position in the school.

REFERENCES

[1] Assembly is often referred to in the text because teachers are more familiar with the term but, strictly speaking, the term 'collective worship' should always be used.

[2] Education Reform Act (ERA) section 7(3).

[3] ERA section 7(1).

[4] ERA section 7(2).

[5] DES Circular 3/89 'The Education Reform Act 1988: Religious Education and Collective Worship', Paragraph 34.

[6] ERA section 6(5).

[7] ERA section 6(3).

[8] ERA section 12(1).

[9] ERA section 11(1)(2).

[10] The fourth committee should appropriately reflect the principal religious traditions in the area. The Free Church Federal Council has issued a report (1989) claiming that LEAs are more concerned to make this committee representative of all faiths than of faiths in their area.

[11] The full details of SACRE are given in sections 11 and 12 of the ERA.

[12] ERA section 9(3).

[13] ERA section 6(2).

[14] ERA section 8(4), (5), (6), (7).

[15] There is, in fact, no agreed definition of worship: it can be narrow, of distinctive acts, or broad, of orientation; it can refer to a personal God or to a trans-personal state; it can refer to awareness, expression, commitment. In short, 'worship' is what it means to those who describe themselves as worshippers.

[16] ERA section 6(3).

[17] Examples such as these and further information on this theme can be found in M Palmer and E Bisset, *World of Difference* published by Blackie for the World Wildlife Fund (ISBN 0 216 91666 6) and the same authors have worked with the Pictorial Charts Education Trust (27 Kirchen Road, West Ealing, London W13 0UD) to produce a set of small posters on 'Creation Stories' which can be used for display purposes.

[18] Commission for Racial Equality, 10/12 Allington Street, London SW1E 5EH.

[19] Martin Palmer, *Faiths and Festivals*, Ward Lock Education,

[20] *Living Festival Series*, Religious and Moral Education Press, Hennock Road, Exeter, EX2 8RP

[21] *The Seder Handbook*, Board of Deputies of British Jews, Woburn House, Upper Woburn Place, London, WC1H 0ED

[22] At a meeting held between ILEA RE Inspectors and the General Secretary of the Association of Christian Teachers, this whole area was explored. Concern had been expressed about the making of a video in an ILEA school in which children 'participated' in a Hindu act of worship. It was noted at the meeting that problems of participation are sometimes compounded by other problems relating to some parents' disapproval of dance and drama and their children's involvement in drama which represents unsavoury characters or wrong actions. Some parents were concerned that knowledge about other faiths will produce changes in their own children.

It is the intention of most RE teachers to reduce prejudice: might this not increase it? It was also recognized that there are differences of theological perspective among Christians so that what might be 'right' for some Christians would be 'wrong' for others. Those Christians who believe in the presence of real (alien) spirits in what to them is pagan religion, believe that their children could be affected; but not all Christians share this view. They would be the 'weak' and 'strong' Christians of Roman 14 and 1 Corinthians 8.

Those Christians whose background and form of worship find ritual to be highly significant are less likely to approve of involvement in an 'act' than those who believe that the significance is not in ritual but in personal commitment. (This divide is very real. A Christian of Baptist persuasion will claim that baptism of infants is not baptism at all because the importance lies not in the ritual but in the personal commitment.) Those Christians who believe that, because we are in a multi-faith society, there is a need to stand up for their faith and to stand out against other faiths are less likely to let their children participate than those who have no such convictions.
[23] Margaret Donaldson, *Children's Minds*, Fontana/Open University
[24] Stories of 'The Life of the Prophet Muhammad' are told by Leila Assam and Aisha Gouverneur in the book published by the Islamic Texts Society. Books of stories from Judaism are available from Rabbi Douglas Charing at the Jewish Educational Bureau, 8 Westcombe Avenue, Leeds, LS8 2BS, by mail order. Macdonald Educational have produced a series of hardback books with 'Stories from the Sikh World' and the worlds of Christianity. Hinduism, Judaism and Islam, but the best way is always to compile a book of stories for use in your own school with the help of children and parents. Over the years it will become a treasured book to use in assembly. Such stories do not always have to come from sacred books. The Narnia Fables by C.S. Lewis and many others from contemporary fiction have a spiritual message as the authors search for meaning.
[25] HMSO, 1985, Page 32.
[26] Harper and Row, US

ACTIVITIES

● Twelve types of assembly are suggested in this section. Can you suggest two additional ones for the 'broadly Christian' assemblies and two for those which are not?
● Start a school book of stories for assembly.
● Draw up an assembly plan for a half term, referring to the Shap Calendar. Use titles for each week and indicate which of these might be done each day.

PART TWO
The Wider Context

5

MORAL EDUCATION AND RE

There are always a number of 'matters arising'—areas that need to be worked through—once people have a general understanding of Religious Education at the primary stage. The purpose of this section is to look at some of these areas.

There has always been an important relationship between religion and morality and some people have therefore made a connection between Religious Education and Moral Education (ME). They have assumed that because morality is one of the outworkings of religion, and because religion is one of the motivation systems for morality, that if children receive Religious Education the moral spin-off will be, for example, less hooliganism at football matches and a better world in which to live.

When debates of this kind are entered into in Parliament, such convictions are often aired. Indeed, one of the factors that led to the initial statutory position of RE in the curriculum, and the later strengthening of its position in the Education Reform Act, was the belief that religion produced the moral goods. Indeed the 'moral argument' is often heard in justification of curriculum time for RE (see chapter 2).

This view has caused teachers a lot of anxiety. There are many misunderstandings or false assumptions. The assumption is made that one cannot be moral without being religious. This is a libel on Humanists, for example, who base their morality on the nature of humanity rather than on revelation in Scripture. There are two other related false assumptions—that the purpose of Religious Education is not to teach children about religions but to make them religious; and that having made a child religious there will be a moral outcome. Both assumptions are false; the first because it is not the purpose of RE in the County School to make anyone religious; the second because religion does not always lead to morality. Indeed, as many people without a religious faith will point out, Christians frequently fail to behave in a 'Christian' way. This is nothing new. In his New Testament letter, James had to point out to people who claimed to be Christian that 'faith without works is dead'.[1]

The root of the problem lies in the fact that belief is only the first step in becoming a Christian. It is what a person does because of their belief which shows whether that person is really a Christian. James pointed out that to believe in God does not make anyone better than a devil, because presumably devils believe in God![2] To be a Christian is to receive the spirit of Jesus into one's life, to give the direction and dynamic which was part of his life, on the basis of the belief that he can and will do this. Paul put it this way: 'If any man has not the spirit of Christ that man is not a Christian'.[3]

This short excursus into Christian theology indicates that people may seem to be Christians because of what they profess, but they are not Christians simply because they live a moral life. To know about the Christian faith, or even to believe some part of it, gives no automatic moral imperative. What is true of Christianity is true of other religious faiths. Simply to know about a religion, without an inner commitment and a changed lifestyle, will not produce such a change in a person.

There is another level of anxiety. Some teachers express the fear that if religion and morality are too closely linked children who come to the point of dropping religion will drop morality too. But such a view is laden with unacceptable value judgments. It is assumed, for example, that while it does not matter if a child rejects religion, it matters a great deal if moral standards are rejected!

Let us assume that because of the distinctiveness of morality and religion (they overlap but are entirely separate) we can treat morality separately and ask how Moral Education might be brought about. This may not be part of RE but it is an area of concern to those involved in RE, as well as to teachers in other curriculum areas. Before we can do this we need to be clear about what we mean by morality.

Clearly there are areas of disagreement about the meaning of morality. Even within a single faith there can be disagreement. Some Christians, for example, will allow abortion under special circumstances and others will not allow it at all; some Christians believe that a nuclear deterrent should be maintained while others believe that even the use of conventional arms is wrong.

But there are many areas where believers of the same faith, and of different faiths, are completely in agreement. These areas correspond to similar moral beliefs held by people with no religious faith. The areas of agreement are normally referred to as 'consensus morality' and usually consist of two areas—human solidarity and personal autonomy. Human solidarity refers to the need to consider others, to understand the importance of their needs and feelings and to offer appropriate help. Personal autonomy refers to the notion that every individual is important and should have the freedom to be him/herself and that no one should be exploited. Consensus morality, therefore, is what we are normally talking about when we refer to Moral Education. We are now in a position to ask how this might be brought about.

The approach to ME: formal or informal?

The first area of the discussion is whether the method should be formal or informal; whether there should be a 'Moral Education' slot in the timetable or whether Moral Education should pervade the whole life of the school. When the old 'Schools' Council' became involved in Moral Education, McPhail, who undertook much of the work, found that the only kind of Moral Education which actually made sense to children was that of considerate lifestyle. When children actually stated what they meant by morality it was taking other people's views, feelings and interests into consideration as well as their own. McPhail produced classroom materials which could be used to develop such sensitivities. He suggested that if children received pleasurable results from showing sensitivity the behaviour would be reinforced and would be more likely to continue.[4] The materials called 'Startline' and 'Lifeline' have largely disappeared from the classroom, but the principles are often taken up within English lessons, where stories and drama set out the situations which lead to increased sensitivity to the needs of others.

Such a structured approach is quite different from that put forward by Loukes. He, too, based his thinking upon observations in the classroom.[5] He went into Oxfordshire schools to talk to teenagers about moral values and found that, by this stage, most knew what they meant by a 'good person'. The teenagers knew how to relate ethical principles to problem situations. But formal, structured ME did not exist in the schools. What he did find in each school was an attempt to prevent corrupting influences, and an attempt to communicate values in the way that children were treated by teachers, in the way they were allowed to participate in the running of the school, in the involvement of parents and in the development of a fair disciplinary system.

Loukes' findings show that Moral Education is bound up with the 'hidden curriculum' and that a child's attitude to moral standards and practice are affected by the way she/he sees such things as selection, pastoral care, organization of group activities, rules, rewards, punishment and community services. The truth of the matter probably lies in a combination of both approaches. All concepts result from language and experience. Formal methods, such as those suggested by McPhail, provide the theoretical language and experience, while school ethos and practice produces the practical language and experience. When both combine to promote consideration, respect for others and 'love for your neighbour' there will be a positive influence on the child.

The content of ME

The second area for discussion is a more detailed look at the language and experience children are to receive. Important work has been done by Wilson[6] to show that there are many components of moral behaviour and that unless one acquires skills in the various components, moral behaviour will not be possible. Moral Education, therefore, becomes a means of training children in those skills which will make moral decisions possible. Wilson invented his own terminology for the components he identified:

Phil—the ability to identify with others
Emp—the ability to understand feelings. (*Autemp*—one's own feelings, and *Allemp*—the feelings of others)
Gig—the necessary knowledge of consequences of actions.

When a person has these basic skills, it is possible to combine them so that rules for behaviour can be made. But this involves other skills:

Dik—the ability to combine basic skills to form rules in relation to others
Phron—the ability to act on principles (since principles of action have to be acted upon too).

Training in the skills comes through discussion, experience, imaginary situations and role play. Hirst, a rationalistic philosopher, used different terms to describe the experiences children should receive.[7] He said that to be moral a person must have procedural knowledge (a knowledge of how to make rational judgments and to exercise social skills) and propositional knowledge (a knowledge of what is involved—the progress being made, of the physical world, of other people, etc). Further a person needs the disposition to think and act rationally and the emotional experiences which will lead to the development of feelings that they will support judgments.

Nottingham put forward a similar idea,[8] but again in different language—that of decision-making skills. He says that moral actions are, in effect, decisions. Therefore Moral Education will proceed as children learn to make decisions. Children are trained by being put into situations in which decisions have to be made so that they have the experience of bringing values and information together. What children learn from making decisions and understanding the consequences will help them when further values and information are brought together to make decisions. Most teachers will recognize that the insights of the academics are correct. There are countless times when teachers will see children take moral decisions because of particular experiences, and because they have been told stories which convey the kind of information that makes such decisions possible.

The time of ME

The third area for discussion concerns the right time for such training to be given to children. Some teachers will be aware of child development and will try to relate the level of experience to the level of development of the child. There is considerable evidence to suggest that, just as learning in other areas of the curriculum needs to be matched to the development of a child, so Moral Education must be tailored to the child's level of understanding. A child's moral development appears to occur in clearly defined stages. It is important to recognize the stages, not only to avoid expecting too much too early, but also so that reactions to children, particularly in the area of discipline, should be related to development.

Piaget was one of the first academics to recognize stages in the development of morality when working with boys and girls from Geneva.[9] He believed that morality was the application of rules and so studied the way in which children apply rules in playing games. He hoped to find out how all rules, moral rules included, were applied. He found that after an initial period in which there was no understanding of the rules of the game at all (for example, when very young children are given marbles they will do anything with them except play a proper game) there followed clearly defined stages. There was a stage when children obeyed the rules which were laid down by adults, but they then moved on to a stage where they agreed with other children what the rules of the game should be. Finally a stage was reached where children made up their own rules and imposed them upon others. The research appears rather weak; not only is it simply descriptive, but many people would agree that rules of games cannot be applied to moral rules. Many, therefore, consider the study irrelevant.

Piaget's work, however, received remarkable confirmation from research undertaken by Bull.[10] He asked West Country children what behaviour they would expect of people in a number of different situations; for example, how they would behave if they saw a child in difficulties in deep water. Bull also observed three stages. There was a stage where children acted to conform to the demands of adults, a stage where children agreed together on an appropriate behaviour, and a stage where children made their own decisions on the basis of what they believed to be right, i.e. right is what adults say is right, then what the group says is right, and ultimately what I know to be right. He described the three stages as heteronomy, socionomy and autonomy. Bull put forward evidence to show that the 'higher' stages cannot be entered into until the lower stages have been passed through; that moral growth depends upon certain previous experiences. He also claimed that it was necessary to relate reactions to children's behaviour to their particular stage of development. Reward and punishment were appropriate to the first stage, praise and blame to the second stage and reasoned argument to the third stage—an interesting comment in the light of current discussion about discipline in school.

Kohlberg took the developmental approach further by looking at the *reasons* children gave for behaviour, rather than descriptions of expected behaviour.[11] Again he noticed three basic stages. However, shrewder analysis enabled him to see two successive components to each stage. The steps are:

Pre-conventional
- Physical consequences of action are crucial—particularly punishment and deference to superior power.
- Satisfaction of personal needs; others are valued for the way they meet our needs.

Conventional
- Good behaviour is what is approved by others.
- Right behaviour is doing one's duty, maintaining the given social order.

Post-conventional
- Social contract; right action is conformity to general rules and standards which have been agreed by others.
- Conscience and self chosen ethical principles.

Kolberg found that all individuals in all cultures and religions go through this sequence. Each step in development has a better cognitive organization than the step before it; one which takes account of everything present in the present stage but makes new distinctions and organizes them into a more comprehensive structure. Development takes place when a child is confronted by the views of another child one step further along. This is very close to the stages of faith and grows from one stage to another as outlined by Fowler (see chapter 4 under *Spiritual development assemblies*). Moral Education therefore becomes a means of challenging the position a child currently holds with the position one stage beyond it. This will come about in utilizing the elements which have been identified by the analytical philosophers, formally and informally throughout the school.[12]

REFERENCES

[1] New Testament: James 2:17.

[2] NT: James 2:19.

[3] NT: Romans 8:9.

[4] P McPhail, D Middleton, D Ingram, *Startline: Moral Education in the Middle Years*, Longman.

[5] N Loukes, *Teenage Morality*, SCM Press.

[6] J Wilson, 'What is Moral Education?' in *Introduction to Moral Education*, Penguin, 1967.

[7] P Hirst, *Moral Education in a Secular Society*, ULP, 1974.

[8] Bermand Nottingham was lecturing on behalf of the Social Morality Council's Moral Education Resource Centre at St Martin's College of ME, Lancaster.

[9] J Piaget, *The Moral Judgment of a Child*, Routledge and Kegan Paul, 1932.

[10] N Bull, *Moral Judgment from Childhood to Adolescence*, Routledge and Kegan Paul, 1969.

[11] L Kohlberg, 'The Child as a Moral Philosopher', *Psychology Today* (2(4)27) 1968.

[12] Teachers involved in current research in education will be aware that this outline is superficial. Those who are interested to follow up the thinking might find M Grimmit, *Religious Education and Human Development*, useful in relating RE to Personal, Social and Moral Education.

6

RE IN THE NURSERY SCHOOL

The Education Reform Act (1988) did not make Religious Education compulsory for children in nursery schools and in nursery classes.[1] Many teachers, however, believe that RE is necessary in the foundation provided during education in the early years, just as foundations are needed in any other curricular area. This conviction grew in Inner London as the result of the work of Penny Lewis. As Nursery Advisory Teacher, she was seconded to the RE team to stimulate work in RE in the nursery phase and to help teachers to understand what was required. The following material, prepared by Penny Lewis, may overlap occasionally with what has been said elsewhere, but to delete any of it would weaken the thrust of her argument.

RE in the nursery curriculum

Many people dismiss Religious Education in the nursery curriculum as being of little value. Religious Education is often approached with diffidence, born of a genuine desire not to confuse or indoctrinate the child, and from the view that religious thought and practices are essentially individual and private. Certainly, the view that children of nursery age are too young to appreciate Religious Education is widespread. If Religious Education is contained exclusively in a narrow, formalized framework, this view would be valid. However, Religious Education is not about indoctrinating children into a particular faith system; it is about how people relate to one another. RE is concerned with how we respond to the world around us and how we respect those things in life entrusted to us, how we view questions of meaning, how we live and how we die. Religious Education encompasses the broad spectrum of practice and ideology operating in modern society.

It is a fact that many of our laws, much of our culture, writings and language are based on religion. Religious thought is part of daily life and part of the cultural identity of many people. We are aware, as educators, that young children constantly work to bring meaning and sense to what they experience. The fact that very young children have neither the vocabulary nor experience adequately to express their feelings of wonder, mystery or awareness does not mean that they are uninterested in nor unaware of the nature of the deity to which they may be exposed; nor that these feelings are not experienced intensely at times. The importance of early stirrings of, what might be termed, an inner spiritual awareness must not be minimised or disregarded.

Very often the capabilities and potential of young children are underestimated. Explicit religious teaching is difficult to understand and little research has been undertaken in determining how far this type of teaching would be appropriate for the nursery child. The research to date—notably by Bruner, Dearden, Donaldson and others—shows that, given an environment and language meaningful to them, very young children can perform tasks and grasp ideas often thought to be beyond them. Of course there are developmental limits, but as educators we are working to provide a stimulating environment so that limits to the whole development of the child can be pushed back. Religious or spiritual growth is not something separate from the rest of the developmental process. Consequently, Religious Education should not occupy the place of 'tail-end Charlie' in our thinking.

There are many facets to nursery education. An underlying principle of nursery provision is that children have considerable control over their learning. In other words, learning is seen as arising out of the needs and interests of the child—not necessarily imposed from outside the child's experience. It is important to note, therefore, that Religious Education at this stage will be implicit in all that we do—part of the continuing development of, and exploration by, the child. Nevertheless, we must also be aware that development as an aim can be seen as 'woolly', with no precise definition or end.

Aims, both in Religious Education and nursery practice, are important. The teacher should be able to identify the religious strands that lie behind the experiences children are encouraged to explore, even though explicit religious teaching is unlikely to be realized for some considerable time. Ideas of awe, wonder, joy and mystery do not 'just happen'—they need to be built up and developed. If this is not encouraged, the more complex Religious Education offered at later stages of schooling will be harder to appreciate and more open to misunderstanding.

In my view there are certain core experiences that we all need if religious concepts and ideas are to be appreciated. Primarily, it is important for the young child to develop trust. Trust in one's environment is a prerequisite to trust in oneself and one's own capabilities. Children also need to know that they are loved and appreciated for what they are.

Trust is not far from faith. Trust in one's own value and worth and trust in others is the cornerstone on which a faith to live by can be built—or the freedom to reject any faith system. This is because a confident person is not threatened or belittled by the choices and evaluations faced in later years. Leading on from this are experiences of relationships, the resolving of difficulties and the space to grow as a unique and individual personality. We need constantly to find ways of building and consolidating these experiences in classroom practice.

Religious Education and other nursery curriculum areas

Given that children are active participants in their own learning, there is a need to view Religious Education not as a separate subject area, but as part of the whole curriculum approach to education. The nursery setting is rich in opportunity for this. There is no area of nursery practice which does not lend itself to the fulfilling of religious objectives; the whole curriculum approach presents varied opportunities for creative and positive Religious Education in the classroom. The following ideas are intended as suggestions of how this might work in practice, together with some pertinent questions to help evaluate practice and the activities offered.

● **Outdoor play** Opportunities abound to study plants, small creatures, spiders' webs hung with dew or rain, snow, puddles, the rainbow and many other things—all of which stimulate a deepening fascination with the world in children. This leads towards building concepts of awe and wonder and to work on life-cycles which help children to pattern their experiences and extend their awareness that life is constantly changing.

Learning to share toys and equipment, to collaborate together in play, being encouraged to try new physical challenges in use of climbing and structural equipment, being aware of the needs of others in turn-taking/sharing activities, and caring for toys because others want to use them, all build a deepening sensitivity to the needs and feelings of others and of personal responsibility in meeting those needs. Very often the sharing of space and staff with other children sees the beginning of developing a personal moral response to others.

● **Scientific exploration** Many activities connected with scientific exploration link with work done in outdoor play. In exploring natural science, the use of equipment such as magnifiers, prisms, reflections and mirror work (together with drawing materials and books readily accessible for close observation work), enhances the children's exploration of the environment and helps in their understanding of the need to be responsible and take care of it.

The nursery should confirm and reflect the experiences children have in society. Technical, scientific exploration is a major part of preparation for the future. Young children are intensely curious about their environment and delight in the opportunity to find out how things work, how they are constructed. Old telephones, radios and torches can be dismantled and handled together with the opportunity to reconstruct, invent and initiate. As well as helping the children in their social development, some teachers may see something of an emotional input here. Many children, as well as adults, transfer what they learn in a physical situation to their internal world and this becomes part of their understanding of what happens around them in relationships. Thus, the child who is given the opportunity to reassemble something which he/she has pulled apart—or the understanding that something broken can be mended—also practices the notion that relationships and feelings can be mended if we take responsibility and work at it. Others may find that link hard to appreciate, but certainly it is true that everything we do and offer a child has some bearing on the whole development of the child.

A topic on food presents many opportunities for exploring religious ideas as well as being rich in educational and social experiences for young children. The topic itself will be of great interest and significance to children. The flow chart shows a variety of ideas, not necessarily to be explored at the same time. However, in just one or two aspects many strands can be incorporated which broaden the experience of the children.

● **Books, stories and pictures** Religious education is about making sense of experience. A story which children find meaningful will provide a starting-point for discussion, for stimulating questions about meaning, and creating a deeper awareness of the needs and feelings of others.

Young children learn a great deal about the world through looking at pictures. Staff working with children can provide pictures which give positive messages about the world and each individual's place within it. The picture content can be related to aspects of cognitive development as well as stimulating thought, language and questioning. Children should be actively encouraged to question the content and message of the picture.

What is happening in this picture? What are the people doing? Why? What will happen if. . . ? How do you think they are feeling—happy, sad, cross? These are the kinds of questions that will stimulate children to think about what they are seeing.

General, non-fiction, books commonly in use in the nursery should be utilized as well as story books—cookery books, science books (life-cycles, growing seeds) etc. Children should also be encouraged to make their own books, for example:

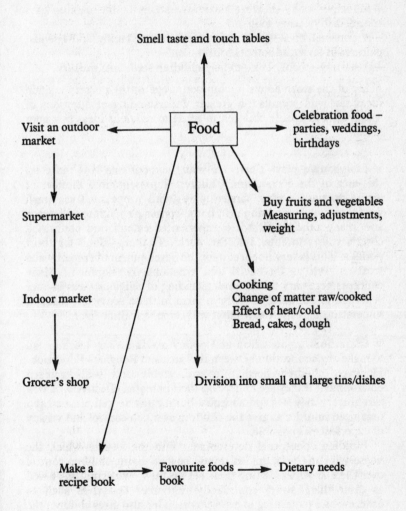

—An activity book—showing different ways in which children have developed a special activity.

—A recipe book—showing successive stages in the making of a special dish or party food.

—A personal book—photo of myself, home, family and friends, pictures of favourite activities and so on.

—A starting school book—to help children settle into nursery.

Many of the story books in common usage in the nursery contain ideas that will stimulate a greater understanding of questions of meaning, and enable children to relate to religious ideas at a later stage.

● **Imaginative play**—There are many components that make up this area of the curriculum. Children 'represent' in a number of ways—drama/role play, fantasy play (with props such as 'small world' toys or by dressing up), home-corner play, mime and dance and many others. All these experiences extend and confirm a child's ability to enter into the world of others—albeit for short periods. This is very important for the development of empathy and trust as well as for social and emotional development. Many concepts necessary for the understanding of religious ideas in later years are to be found in embryo form in these activities; seeds of understanding will be sown that will come to fruition later.

● **Classroom organization and policy making** Many teachers fail to make any connection between this area and Religious Education. However, children need a secure, stable and well-organized environment if they are to develop their potential effectively. A well run nursery may *look* spontaneous, but it must be well planned and organized in order to give the children as much control and variety of experience as possible.

Building conceptual development into the way in which the nursery is run (bays, graded storage spaces, giving children control over their activities, letting them set up their own activities as well as clear them away) continually reinforces objectives such as ordering and patterning of experiences. This also gives children the opportunity to initiate and collaborate with one another. It provides children with the opportunity to develop decision making skills leading to choice.

Policy making—the handling of disputes, personal relationships between staff members as well as between staff and parents, and staff and children—is of vital importance. The so called 'hidden curriculum' teaches children much about respect for other people, for the differences between them. It teaches them to be tolerant of others and to respect their worth and value as individuals. It is in the nursery ethic that the foundations for responsibility to self and others are laid.

Working within the nursery phase is a demanding and very rewarding experience. If the aim is to foster a fruitful learning environment where all children and their families feel valued and involved, it is necessary that educators positively recognize, and draw on, the cultural and faith resources of every child.

Nursery education should have the strongest links with the community. Continuity of experience for children and their families can lay positive foundations for future attitudes and the development of the whole person. In the nursery, Religious Education should be based on respect for what children and their families bring to the school experience. It should provide good foundational experience on which further stages of Religious Education can be built right through the education process. We need to ensure that the foundations laid in early childhood are strong and positive, enabling our children to move towards maturity confident and secure in themselves so that they can take their place creatively in modern society.

REFERENCES

[1] ERA Section 25(2): Nothing in this chapter ("The Curriculum", which includes provision for RE) shall apply in relation to a nursery school or a nursery class in a primary school.

7

ASSESSMENT IN RELIGIOUS EDUCATION

When Government implemented its policies through the Education Reform Act, its concern for consistency and high standards was incorporated into new arrangements for assessment. All subjects within the National Curriculum have to work to attainment statements which set out what level of knowledge, understanding and skills should be expected at the end of each *key stage* in education—7, 11, 14 and 16.

In addition to this, attainment targets are to be set for each year, so that pupils and teachers can know what is expected from year to year. These statements and targets are agreed at national level. When attainment targets are grouped together to form the major components of a subject area, they are referred to as profile components and are intended to form the basis of reports to parents. The 'matters, skills and processes' to be taught to enable pupils to reach the attainment targets are referred to as 'programmes of study' and the means of assessing how far pupils and teachers have met the targets are referred to as 'assessment arrangements'.

Religious Education is left out of this attainment assessment procedure because it is not part of the National Curriculum; the National Curriculum plus RE constitutes the basic (compulsory) curriculum. Government has made it possible for RE to be included, but has not made it compulsory. The reason was that there is no National Curriculum in operation for RE because RE is locally-determined through the local Agreed Syllabus Conference. Government, therefore, left it with the local Agreed Syllabus Conference to decide whether or not it wanted RE to be assessed in the same way as other subjects. (In fact the law does not say that this has to be done by the Agreed Syllabus Conference; there seems to be no reason why this should not be done by a Standing Advisory Committee on RE—SACRE).[1]

This situation has led to a lot of heart searching. There are many people, particularly in the voluntary sector, where RE sometimes has a purpose beyond education about religion, who have felt that assessment detracts from the special nature of RE because there are attitudes and inner responses which are not subject to assessment. There are also many teachers in primary schools who, aware of the many subject areas they are involved in, do not welcome the prospect of one more for assessment.

On the other hand there are people, particularly in the secondary sector of education in County Schools, who feel that if RE is not assessed in the same way as other subjects it will rapidly be downgraded. This view has been taken by the Religious Education Council, a multi-faith organization that represents all bodies concerned about RE in the country, and by the National Association of RE Advisers and Inspectors. Both organizations have set up working parties to test the feasibility of assessment in RE. They have been able to do this because the various Agreed Syllabuses have so much in common that there is almost a national syllabus for RE in existence anyway. Certainly this is true for 14–16-year-olds, where the national criteria for the GCSE examination operate.

This has been taken much further by a consortium of twenty-nine LEA's working with the Midlands Regional RE Centre at Westhill College in Birmingham. A working party has produced a handbook called 'Attainment in RE' which includes ten attainment targets under three profile components and examples of content which can be related to the attainment targets at each of the four key stages: 4–7, 7–11, 11–14, and 14–16. It is an excellent piece of work.[2]

When a working party of the ILEA SACRE looked into this, they believed that what was unique and special about RE was its concepts or areas of meaning. Skills and attitudes were an important part of RE but they were not unique to RE; rather they were skills and attitudes shared with other subject areas and applied to religion. This did not mean that skills and attitudes were irrelevant but that together with understanding they constituted ways by which the attainment of concepts might be tested. Let us break this down a little:

Concepts

Upon examination it was felt that the ideas, concepts, or areas of meaning of religion were the unique ingredient of RE in a County School because worship, prayer and meditation are appropriate only in some Voluntary (Aided) Schools. There were different kinds of concepts.

● **Fundamental concepts** are those which underlie religious understanding. They are not necessarily religious but without them religious understanding cannot proceed. Fundamental concepts include ideas such as 'person' and 'relationships' and are linked to the area of RE described as implicit (see chapter 2).

● **Linguistic concepts** are those which are involved in the naming of religious things and are normally specific to each religion. 'Font' and 'Eucharist' are examples of such words in a Christian context, 'Mishnah' and 'Mezuzah' in the Jewish context; 'Eid' and 'Salat' in an Islamic context.

● **Contextual concepts** are those which enable us to put a particular word or idea in its place. Long ago Ninian Smart identified what he called the 'dimensions of religion' which are common to all and can be used as a means of describing any religion. They are 'doctrine', 'myth', 'ethic', 'ritual', 'experience', 'social expression'. When these ideas are understood it becomes possible to classify other words or ideas accordingly, so that for example the word 'circumcision' is put into the category of 'ritual'.

● **Theological concepts** are those which are common to many religions and are therefore characteristic of religion itself. These are words/ideas such as 'revelation', 'sacred', 'soul' and 'providence'.

The ideas can probably be grouped about central ideas such as authority, belief, God, lifestyle, ultimate questions, value and spirituality (which at secondary phase level are the clusters of concepts which a GCSE group put forward as the central areas of study for RE).

• **Relational concepts** are other areas with which religion is related, such as sociology, history, science and politics. We have to understand what these words stand for in order to understand how religion relates to each area of study.

The interesting thing about this list of concepts is that the groups are in a rough chronological order of attainment/appearance, although there is a lot of overlap. Some people have related these to the five key stages—in RE there is a fifth stage, 16–18. The fundamental concepts are often linked to the infant phase of RE, the linguistic concepts are linked both at infant and junior level, and so on. Growth in understanding particular ideas will occur. There is growth in sophistication, detail, subtlety, complexity, abstraction and sensitivity.

Assessment

How can we assess whether these concepts have been attained? Understanding, skills and attitudes are all involved and these are the tools of assessment. Finding out whether a child has understanding or skills or attitudes is a means of testing for concept formation. A list of areas concerned with understanding skills and attitudes constitutes an RE 'field' or 'map'.

What do we expect pupils to understand? An analysis of syllabuses indicates there are seven areas of implicit/foundational RE and seven areas of explicit RE.

Implicit RE understanding includes understanding of self and others (identity, relationships, development and growth), greatness (awe and wonder, mystery), pleasure (happiness, delight, enjoyment), sorrow (support in times of fear, sorrow and suffering), peace/love (tranquillity), integrity (right and wrong, consistency, order and pattern) and representation (expressive and performing arts, symbol and writing). Compare this list with the primary objectives set out in chapter 1. It has been necessary to include the bracketed words because single words are not in themselves adequate to define the whole area of meaning; the single words are 'pegs' for a group of ideas.

Explicit RE understanding includes understanding of activities (worship and ritual/rites, festivals/fasts, celebrations), beliefs/ideas (what is true—theology, what is right—ethics, what should be done —practice), experience (commitment, relationships, attitudes), history (events, places, people), organization (authority-scripture, traditions and people, organizations, institutions, buildings), people (founders, figures, followers) and writings (books, literature, stories, language and symbol). Again, look at the list of primary objectives in chapter 1.

We can assess whether or not there has been understanding in these areas by using questions or giving directions which involve words like 'know', 'understand', 'discuss', describe', 'recount', 'explain', 'be aware of' and 'tell'. We should be able to make attainment statements like, 'understand how and why the cross is used as a symbol in Christianity', or (much wider), 'know the stories which lie behind some festivals'.

We can also use skills which children have already learned to test how far concepts have been achieved. There is a group of skills related to the observation and recording of religion—learning what to look for (recall), recognizing the significance of what is seen and knowing how to go about investigating religion. Another group of skills is related to the formulation, classifying and sequencing of information. This includes the ability to ask the right questions, the ability to reflect on experience and the ability to assess the impact of religion.

The third group of skills concerns communication about religion and involves description and discussion, the use of symbolic language, the ability to enter into another person's experience imaginatively and the ability to enter into dialogue.

None of these skills is unique to RE, but when they are applied to religious material their right use is an indication that the material has been rightly understood. Assessment statements will use words such as 'recall', 'recognize', 'investigate', 'ask', 'research', 'inter-view', 'observe' and so on. Assessment statements might include 'be able to interview a believer about his/her faith and write a coher-ent account of his/her basic beliefs'.

We can look at attitudes to see if concepts are being achieved. Is there an interest in religion? Does the child want to know more about religion? Does the child show an appropriate sense of responsibility, taking notice of things which need to be taken account of such as law and order, health, safety, and other people's interests? Is the child sensitive, appreciating other people's feelings, taking note of things in a considerate way and responding in an appropriate manner? Assessment statements might include 'show-ing sensitivity to other people's feelings when talking about things of importance to them', or 'actively concerning himself or her-self with personal cleanliness in accordance with the tenets of his family faith'.

This results in twenty-one areas through which the attainment of concepts might be assessed—rather more than some people would have hoped for—but comprehensive because they include the implicit areas of Religious Education (which many people seem to have forgotten) as well as the explicit and skills and attitudes as well as understanding. It is important that these areas reflect concepts fundamental to religion and that they are capable of being applied to any religions which are studied.

The list of twenty-one areas is inadequate to express exactly what is meant and each one has to be written out in full. The area of explicit understanding of people might be written as follows:

'Pupils should recognize the importance of people in the story of religion so that they know about those who have founded religious faiths and those who have continued them. They should know the stories of their lives against the historical and cultural background and be able to give an account of some of their followers where they have been significant in propagating, influencing or demonstrating the faith'.

Beyond this it is necessary to write, first a set of attainment statements for each area on the map for guidance of teachers and pupils at 7, 11, 14 and 16 years, and then to refine this further into attainment targets for each year. At the time of writing, consideration of how this is to be done and how achievement of the targets should be assessed is just beginning.[3] It will be a lengthy task and, where adopted, will influence the actual structure of the Agreed Syllabus.[4]

REFERENCES

[1] Circular 3/89, Paragraph 20 says: 'A Conference established by a local education authority . . . to review a locally agreed syllabus may recommend the inclusion of attainment targets, programmes of study and assessment arrangements in locally determined form in their proposals.'

[2] The AREAI report 'Religious Education for Ages 5 to 16/18' can be obtained from the RE/ME Enquiry Service at St Martins College, Lancaster LA1 3JD. The Westhill Report 'Attainment in RE' can be obtained from the Regional RE Centre (Midlands), Westhill College, Selly Oak, Birmingham B29 6LL.

[3] This is much more open to development than at first believed. It looks as though assessment materials will be given to teachers rather than teachers having to develop the assessment materials. At key stage four, a modified form of GCSE might be used. Standard Assessment Tasks might prove to be so time consuming that they affect teaching time. Only when these things become certainties will progress be made.

[4] There are problems here. Government was advised that assessment should be formative—that is, able to be used to devise a future relevant programme of work for an individual child. But Government tends towards the view that it should be summative—summing up on all a child has attained. Again, Parliament was advised that teachers should be involved in devising and operating The Standard Achievement Tasks but Government tends to the view that teachers should not be involved. These issues are still to be resolved.

8

PROBLEMS OF CONSCIENCE IN TEACHING RE

Religion has always thrown up problems of conscience. There are things which people cannot, or will not, do because of their faith and there are things which they must do because of their faith. Since parents, teachers and children have all come to, or are coming to, answers which are real to them about the basic issues of existence and because Religious Education deals with such questions there will often be anxiety and even feelings of inner conflict about Religious Education.

Problems for teachers of no faith

Teachers who have no religious faith sometimes feel that they are personally compromised by taking part in Religious Education. If they are teachers in a County School and are not what are called 'reserved' teachers in a Voluntary (controlled) School they have the right of withdrawal from assembly and from Religious Education without being penalized in any way. Section 30 of the 1944 Education Act says:

'No person shall be disqualified by reason of his religious opinions or of his attending or omitting to attend religious worship from being a teacher in a county or voluntary school . . . and no teacher shall be required to give religious instruction or receive any less emolument or be deprived of or disqualified for any promotion or other advantage by reason of the fact that he does or does not give religious instruction or by reason of his religious opinions or of his attending or omitting to attend religious worship.'

119

What is true for teachers is also true for headteachers. The Education Reform Act makes it clear that headteachers have the same right of withdrawal as other teachers but that they still have the responsibility for seeing that the religious provisions of the Acts are carried out in their schools. Circular 3/89 on Religious Education and Collective Worship under the Education Reform Act says in paragraph 47:

'The safeguards (for teachers) apply to Headteachers as to all other teachers. Headteachers have a duty under Section 10 of the Act to see that the law on collective worship and RE is complied with in their school but except (in voluntary aided schools) they cannot be penalised for not taking part in the provision of either.'

I personally, however, find it difficult to understand why a teacher would wish to exercise the right of withdrawal. First, they are not being asked to teach about any religion in a way that inducts children into a faith. Were they being asked to do the work of an evangelist their resistance would be understandable; but in County Schools this is not the case—children are learning about religion.

The reasons why children are taught about religions have already been spelled out—so that they will have information instead of misinformation and so be less prejudiced to those who do not have the same beliefs; so that they can find their way in our culture; and so that they can grow towards personal maturity. It has already been explained how these reasons for RE affect the material which is presented. I cannot imagine why any teacher would not want children to be taught these things. Again, personally speaking, I therefore find it difficult to view withdrawal from the type of 'RE' taught in schools today as anything other than some kind of prejudice.

Problems for teachers of a particular faith

Sometimes strong allegiance to a particular faith places a teacher in a very difficult position. Most teachers who face such problems are Christians and for this reason this section will address itself particularly to their problems; but, of course, the problems are not unique to Christians.

The problems are linked to views of the unique truth claims of their own faith. Although there are many people in the church who look upon all religions as being ways to God, the New Testament has a much narrower view. Jesus himself said, 'I am the way, the truth and the life. No man cometh unto the Father but by me'.[1] In the early preaching of the church it was proclaimed, 'Neither is there any other name under Heaven by which we must be saved'.[2]

Christianity is described here as being the one way to God—ruling out other religions. This kind of outlook is shared with believers from other faiths who also believe that their faith is exclusive. When teachers who hold such views are asked to teach about other (i.e., non-Christian) religions they may know that they are teaching children about religions rather than inducting them into a faith, and they may know that in a multi-faith community it is necessary for the different faiths to receive recognition, but still encounter personal problems.

● **Disobedience** One of these problems is that Christians are called to evangelize and propagate their faith. There is no doubt that this is true. The last thing that Jesus was recorded to have said is that his followers should go out into the world teaching people all that he had commanded them.[3]

But being a sincere Christian in following such an instruction no more means that one has to 'preach the gospel' as a teacher in an RE lesson than it means that a milkman has to 'preach the gospel' as a milkman when delivering milk. If a milkman was to knock at houses at 6 a.m. to say 'Good morning here is your milk, I want to tell you about Jesus' most of the customers would go elsewhere. It is just as inappropriate to 'preach the gospel' in a French lesson or in a geography lesson—and of course in an RE lesson too. There is a right time and place for following this particular commandment and it is not in the RE slot on the timetable. Initially, the best way that the milkman could 'preach the gospel' is living the gospel by being a really superb milkman, sensitive to customers' needs, working without waking people up . . . The best way the Christian teacher can 'teach the gospel' is by aiming to be a really superb teacher.

● **Personal compromise** Another claim is that teaching about other faiths effectively leads to compromise. Christianity differs from other faiths because it is based upon a personal relationship with Jesus Christ. Christians believe that Jesus is alive and well in the twentieth century and that through the Holy Spirit they can enter into a personal relationship with him. Christians believe that he is actually able to help them live their lives to a higher standard than they could without him; that he guides them through the maze of circumstances and decisions which are part of life; that he stabilizes them in difficult situations—the result being a strong, mature love. Christians who feel like this often believe that teaching about other religions is disloyal and that to treat any religion as being equal to Christianity is to compromise.

However, objectivity in the classroom does not mean a teacher has to hide his or her faith or deny or be inconsistent about that faith. It is recognized that teachers cannot be totally objective about their own faith (any more than about other views they hold). It is therefore sometimes suggested that teachers with strong beliefs should make them clear to children. This will mean the teacher is not compromised and it avoids any possibility of children facing some form of indoctrination.

Children need to understand the effects of the exclusive truth claims of religion in the lives of believers and this is a way of helping them to an understanding. The important thing is that the teacher is open. Teachers need to be open so that pupils can make their own assessment of what the teacher says; they also need to be open in terms of listening to other expressions of faith or points of view; finally teachers need to be open in the sense that in addition to being able to say 'I believe this because of A,B and C' they can also say 'this is what someone else believes because of X,Y and Z'.

● **False teaching** There are people who feel that teaching children about something that the teacher believes to be false will cause problems. It either confirms some children who follow that particular path in their error, or else prevents them from coming to the truth as the teacher sees it. Such teachers believe that it is their job to point people to the light and not away from the light. I have sometimes had to say to Christian teachers that such an approach demonstrates a rather high opinion of their ability to persuade or dissuade a person from becoming a Christian. The New Testament not only makes it clear that it is God who takes the initiative in convincing people that it is right for them to follow Jesus, it also makes it clear that it is not possible for human beings to take such a step without the operation of God.

If, despite this attempt to give an apologia for teaching RE, a believer still cannot undertake what is required, there is no question that they have the right of withdrawal from RE. But such a withdrawal is a pity, because believers have so much to offer Religious Education.

Problems for parents

Parents of a particular faith, and parents of no faith, often write to an Education Authority to express their concern about their children having to take RE and attend assembly. Of course they do not 'have to'. Parents have the right to withdraw their children from the whole, or part, of RE and/or assembly. The law as stated in the Education Reform Act Section 9(3) says:

'If a parent of any pupil in attendance of any main school requests that he may be wholly or partly excused;
(a) from attendance at religious worship in the school,
(b) from receiving Religious Education given in the school in accordance with the schools basic curriculum,
(c) both from such attendance and from receiving such education
    the pupil shall be excused accordingly until the request is withdrawn.'

In fact the withdrawal can be quite positive. It can be utilized so that the child can be instructed in his or her own faith. The law says that:

'Where . . . any pupil has been partly or wholly excused from attendance at religious worship or from receiving Religious Education in any school and the responsible authority are satisfied—

(a) that the parent of the pupil desires him to receive religious education of a kind which is not provided in the school during the periods of time during which he is so excused,

(b) that the pupil cannot with reasonable convenience be sent to another maintained school where Religious Education of the kind desired by the parent is provided and,

(c) that arrangements are being made for him to receive religious education of that kind during school hours elsewhere, the pupil may be withdrawn from the school during such periods of time, as are reasonably necessary for the purpose of enabling him to receive Religious Education in accordance with the arrangements' (Education Reform Act Section 9(4)).

The Act goes on to say that such attendance must not interfere with the attendance of the pupil at school on any day except at the beginning or the end of the school session. There is, to my mind, a certain amount of confusion between what the law says and what the subsequent Circular 3/89 says.

It seems possible that children from secondary schools can receive instruction in their own faith on the school premises provided that it does not involve cost to the Local Education Authority or the governors. But there is some confusion as to whether the children can actually join in an act of their own worship.[4]

The worries that parents have reflect the worries that teachers have. These arise in three forms. First there is misunderstanding of the nature of RE. If parents believe that their children are being taught in a way that will lead them to become believers of another faith or life style, they will be reluctant to let their children participate. It therefore needs to be underlined that the purpose of RE and assembly linked to an Agreed Syllabus in a County School is not to induct a child into any faith but to help children understand about a number of faiths, so that they become religiously literate.

Some parents, however, are still anxious. They fear that if children actually learn about other faiths they will become affected by them.

Some parents also fear that a child's own faith will be undermined by looking at faiths one by one and that this will lead the child to believe that all religions are equally true.[5]

Some people have challenged parents who hold this view, asking whether children brought up in a family faith should be denied the right to find a faith for themselves. I understand that thinking— even though I do not agree with it! The point also has to be made, of course, that learning about other faiths does not necessarily weaken one's own. There comes a stage beyond religious literacy where faiths can be seen side by side.

If one looks at one's own beliefs through the eyes of someone of another faith it can clarify issues and lead to a deeper level of understanding. But beyond this, if a person tells me that the faith of their child is likely to be undermined by studying other religions I ask two questions: 'Are you properly fulfilling your responsibility to your child?' and 'What is your faith really worth if it will not stand up against another?'

In the Jewish law it was stated that parents were to talk through their faith with their children.[6] If parents are prepared to talk through their faith with their children, in the light of what their children learn in school, will there be any weakening of the faith of the family? On a personal level, I am convinced that the ultimate truth claims of the faith I hold are such that 'exposure' to any other teaching will not affect them. I therefore have no fear for my own faith nor do I fear the affect on my own children of learning about other faiths.

Parents still voice concern, however, over certain ways of teaching about other faiths—those methods which involve active learning and role play. Children are great pretenders. When they pretend to be a believer in another faith, when they pretend to take part in the festival of another faith, and when they pretend to take part in a ritual, they know that they are pretending and that they have not really become believers, worshippers, or celebrants. It is a game—like doctors and nurses, teachers and headteachers, mummies and daddies—through which they learn. I have not seen any evidence of role play affecting children or turning them into believers. I do accept, however, that there are spiritual realities behind religion; that behind the observance there are real spiritual powers; and I believe that these spiritual realities can bring about an effect in the life of any one who is present.

If a parent does not wish their child to go into a Buddhist temple or take part in a simulated act of Hindu worship I have to respect the wishes of the parent to withdraw their child from that element in RE. There is no clear-cut line which can be drawn for teachers in this. Some parents are more sensitive than others, some have more fundamental beliefs than others. Such sensitivity in parents is not to be challenged, but accepted.

REFERENCES

[1] New Testament: John 14:6.

[2] NT: Acts 4:12.

[3] NT: Matthew 28:18,20.

[4] I feel that there is a certain amount of confusion between what the law says and what has come from the Department of Education and Science in Circular 3/89.

In the 1944 Education Act it was clear that children withdrawn from school could receive religious instruction off the school premises at the beginning and end of the school session provided that it did not interfere with school attendance (section 25(5)). This has been taken over into the Education Reform Act, where 'religious education' replaces 'religious instruction' (section 9(4)).

The 1944 Act went on to say that secondary school pupils could receive that instruction in their own schools if it was more convenient and if no cost fell on the Authority (section 26) and this was taken over in the ERA by schedule I(i) sections (3) and (4).

It is clear that collective worship cannot be arranged for pupils who form a denomination, because no denominational worship may be arranged (ERA section 7(2)) and it is also clear that collective worship may not be celebrated by a religious group because any groups holding collective worship must be of different age groups or school (teaching?)

groups (ERA section 6(2)). This is made explicit in the circular (para.31) where it specifically says that the group 'does not mean a group reflecting particular religious beliefs'.

The wording of the ERA Section 12(2) where it refers to determinations being made by SACRE on behalf of 'any class or description of pupils at such a school' makes it appear that SACRE can determine whether Christian collective worship would be appropriate for such a group (as might be withdrawn), and they can then 'determine the character of the collective worship which is appropriate in their case'.

In view of these statements in law, paragraph 42 in the circular seems incomprehensible when it states 'nothing in the Act prevents any maintained school from allowing, at the request of parents, religious education to be provided, and religious worship to take place according to a particular faith or denomination where parents have withdrawn pupils from the RE or collective worship provided in accordance with the law. The Secretary of State believes that governing bodies and headteachers should seek to respond positively to such request from parents.' There are several conditions—that the 'denominational worship' should not replace statutory non-denominational worship, that it costs nothing and that the overall purpose is consistent with the Act, and these conditions reflect the current legal requirements, but the position taken in the (non-statutory) circular does not seem to say the same thing as the law.

[5] There is a difficulty here: everyone acknowledges that we have to be critical of religion—otherwise Van Daniken would still be in vogue! Most people would be critical of scientology. But where do we stop? Religions have always been critical of each other and all acknowledge the importance of self criticism. Clearly a line has to be drawn but, as yet, nobody knows where.

[6] Old Testament: Deuteronomy 6:4,7.

9

RE IN DIFFERENT TYPES OF SCHOOL

In the course of this book a distinction has often been made between County Schools, Voluntary (Controlled) Schools and Voluntary (Aided) Schools. The distinctions in detail are very complex.[1] The situation arose because when, in 1944, Government wished to provide secondary education for all (i.e. education which was more than 'elementary') there were not enough schools run by Local Authorities to meet the increased numbers of pupils. Christian, Jewish and some independent schools joined in. They were designated as particular types of Voluntary School depending upon how much Government money was put in to maintain the school.

County Schools

County Schools are those set up and maintained by the Local Education Authority.

Aided Schools

Aided Schools are those schools which were previously outside the LEA system and (who currently) contribute 15 per cent of the cost toward external repairs and alterations to the school buildings, the rest coming from Government. The LEA still looks after internal repairs and the school playing field. In return for the 15 per cent contribution, the school has a number of very important advantages:

• Representatives of the church, or body, that founded the school form the majority in the board of governors or managers.

• The governors can use the premises however they like outside school hours.

• The teachers are the employees of the governors and not the Local Education Authority—although the number of teachers is controlled by the Local Authority and salaries are paid by the LEA. The LEA has to authorize the dismissal of a teacher—but not an RE teacher. The governors can dismiss an RE teacher if the teacher does not teach in accordance with the trust deeds of the school.

• The Religious Education given in a Voluntary (Aided) School is determined by the governors and (unless they choose otherwise) is independent of the Local Authority Agreed Syllabus. If, however, the parents of any child at the school wish him/her to receive RE according to the Agreed Syllabus, and there is no other school that the child can attend, the governors have to make arrangements for its provision. Since the Agreed Syllabus is linked to the LEA, if a school does not use it neither LEA Inspector nor Government Inspector (HMI) has the right to carry out any inspection on RE. Inspection is in the hands of the governors. Teachers in an Aided School may be required to teach RE and are not protected from governors acting against them if they refuse to do so.

• Assembly can sometimes take place off the school premises.

Controlled Schools

Controlled Schools are those schools previously outside the LEA system which could not provide the 15 per cent cost of maintenance. The governors are not, therefore, usually responsible for any charges on the school. As a result the school has less freedom than an Aided School.

● The church or body which founded the school is represented on the governing body but is not the majority.

● The governors can use the school premises however they like on Sundays, and on Saturdays provided that the building or field is not needed by the LEA for educational purposes.

● Teachers are employees of the Local Authority, but a few teachers can be appointed as 'reserved teachers' (depending on the size of the school) to teach RE according to the trust deeds. Such RE is not normally taught in a Controlled School because the Agreed Syllabus is used. It is, however, possible for parents to ask for RE to be provided for their child under the trust deeds. The governors have to fulfil this request. If the governors are not happy with the way the 'reserved teacher' has carried out the trust deed's instructions for RE, they can ask the Authority to remove the reserved status so that the teacher stops teaching RE. Reserved teachers in a Controlled School do not have the same protection as other teachers.

● LEA Inspectors and Government Inspectors (HMI) may inspect the Agreed Syllabus RE but arrangements for the inspection of 'trust deed RE' are made by the governors.

● Assembly always take place on the school premises.

Special Agreement Schools

In 1944, when Government was defining types of schools in terms of the (current) 85 per cent or 100 per cent grant for buildings there were some schools which did not fit. In 1936 Local Authorities set up schools together with voluntary bodies, or extended schools that belonged to voluntary bodies in order to prepare for the raising of the school leaving age. The LEA was to provide between 50 per cent and 75 per cent of the capital cost. Very few schools had taken this up before the war, but in 1944 those schools intending to use the 'special agreement' were permitted to revive the agreement and they became known as Voluntary (Special Agreement) Schools. The arrangements made for such schools fall somewhere between those made for Controlled and Aided Schools.

● Arrangements for maintenance and use of buildings are the same as for Aided Schools.

● Arrangements for RE under the trust deeds (and therefore inspection) are the same as for Aided Schools.

● Arrangements for assembly are the same as for Aided Schools.

● But arrangements for appointment of teachers to teach RE are the same as for Controlled Schools.

Under the Education Reform Act all of these provisions have been upheld. Sections 26, 27 and 28 of the 1944 Education Act have been updated in Schedule I of the Education Reform Act but are substantially the same. The big difference between Voluntary Schools and County Schools is over collective worship. Voluntary Schools are not subject to the requirement that most acts of collective worship in any school term must be broadly Christian.

Grant Maintained Schools

A new type of school was established under the new Education Reform Act. These schools, after opting out of Local Authority support, can be maintained by a grant direct from Government.

When a school opts out of an authority, the arrangements for RE and collective worship are normally the same as they were before the opting out. However, at the time it becomes Grant Maintained the governors may wish to change the religious status of the school. If the trustees of the school (if there are any) and the Secretary of State approve the change then the school can alter its religious status and take on the regulations for RE and collective worship appropriate to this status. It is extremely important for religious communities that have become the majority group in a local community that this should be allowed to happen. A County School could, in this way, become effectively a Voluntary (Aided) School under the title or description of a Grant Maintained School. Muslim communities, for example, that have pressed for Voluntary (Aided) Schools with little success might be able to achieve their aims by this means.

If a Grant Maintained School intends using the Agreed Syllabus it must be consulted during discussions of its formulation and Grant Maintained Schools in any LEA are to be represented on SACRE. Grant Maintained Schools, like Aided Schools, may occasionally hold 'collective worship' off the school premises.[2]

SPECIAL EDUCATION

Some people have contacted me to confirm that, under the provisions of the Education Reform Act, they do not have to do RE in Special Schools. It is certainly true that they are not included in the religious provision of the Act. Section 2(3) says that provision for Religious Education for all registered pupils at the school 'shall not apply in the case of a Maintained Special School'. But this is not to do away with RE; RE in the Special Schools comes under a different set of regulations. There are two statements in the law.

The 1983 Education Act (Approval of Special Schools) which was amended by the Education Reform Act (Schedule I(9)) says:

'Provision shall be made in the regulations to secure that, so far as possible, every pupil attending a Special School will attend religious worship and receive Religious Education, or will be withdrawn from attendance at such worship or from receiving such education, in accordance with the wishes of his parent.'

The existing regulations are in Schedule 2(9) of the Education (Approval of Special Schools) Regulations 1983. They say almost exactly the same thing.

'Arrangements shall be made to secure that as far as practicable every pupil attending the school would attend religious worship and religious instruction unless his parent has expressed a wish to the contrary, in which case the pupils should be withdrawn from attendance at such worship or instruction in accordance with that wish.'

It is clear that Special Schools are to follow the same principles for RE and collective worship as every other school, but headteachers are to bear in mind that some children in Special Schools are disadvantaged, so the programme has to be arranged appropriately. This is in line with the Warnock Report (Special Educational Needs)[3] which said that aims for all children, regardless of ability, should be the same. Overall aims in RE will therefore be the same as for any other type of school, though there may be differences in methods of approach and the objectives may be simpler, (related to different ages, and in some cases even omitted).

The following extract from a paper by Jill Davies, Advisory Teacher for RE in Special Education for the ILEA SACRE, published in the second edition of the Authority's Agreed Syllabus, explores the different methods and approaches needed for teaching RE in Special Schools.

'Some aspects of Religious Education, for example an emphasis on abstract concepts, will present special difficulties for some of these pupils, particularly where linguistic development has been impaired. At the same time it has been noted that many may have a particular contribution to make in other areas, for example, of religious experience and intuitive understanding.

'A number of Special Schools serve children who have ability within the normal range. This applies particularly to schools for pupils with sensory impairments, for pupils with emotional and behavioural difficulties, for pupils who have health problems or who did not prosper in ordinary schools, and to schools for pupils with physical disabilities. For such pupils in Special Schools, the objectives for primary and secondary pupils, the suggested topics and how these can be developed, as described in the Agreed Syllabus, are appropriate. Methodologies adopted and the pace of learning expected must take into account the effects of disabilities upon learning. For example, pupils who are blind need time to learn the content of their physical world through sustained opportunities to explore by touch and through careful discussion to ensure true understanding. Children with profound and severe hearing loss, who unlike their hearing peers do not acquire concepts and language incidentally through informal social experience, need much help and time devoted to the acquisition of new concepts in all areas of learning, including Religious Education.

'Children who are emotionally disturbed have often lost confidence in their own abilities, read and write with difficulty and lack motivation for learning. Their teachers will have to work very skilfully to arouse and sustain interest in many areas of learning. Some older emotionally disturbed pupils, and others who suffer from sensory or physical disabilities, may be more inclined to take up polarized attitudes to Religious Education because they are angry about their own condition. These problems, which are inherent in various fields of special education, can be resolved or largely overcome but the time and effort required to achieve the levels reached by non-handicapped pupils must never be underestimated.

'It is the case that many Special Schools have a wider ability range and age distribution than normal schools and are required to provide a modified curriculum for their less able children. The majority of Special Schools serve pupils with moderate or severe learning difficulties. These children's general development has been and will continue to be slower than that of most children. Learning takes place in much smaller steps and, for many, abstract concepts are learned with great difficulty. The slower pace of learning and the limitations to complex learning are especially marked in children who have severe learning difficulties.

'Pupils with moderate learning difficulties need content and methodology which will best support their learning. They will require an emphasis on direct and concrete experience, a focus upon the present and the local with learning reinforced by appropriate repetition. Much use must be made of creative/expressive activities. Because of the slower pace of learning it is likely that less ground will be covered in the Religious Education syllabus. For children with severe learning difficulties no learning will take place if the experience is outside the comprehension level of the child. The teachers of such children are well aware of how young their charges are in developmental terms and of how slow progress will be.

'The school assembly can provide an important focus for the life of the school community within a religious perspective. Imaginatively used, it can celebrate diversity and differences, within a framework which shares positive contributions from children and staff in their work together. It can also offer a forum for the presentation of the creative and expressive activities which will form an essential part of the Religious Education of children in Special Schools.

'It is important for all children, including those in Special Schools, to have access to the broadest possible range of curriculum. The opportunity to look at life from a religious perspective and to understand religious insights is part of the richness which all schools seek to offer to their pupils as a preparation for adult life.'

REFERENCES

[1] See, for example, K Brooksbank, (Society of Education Officers) *County and Voluntary Schools* Councils and Education Press/Longman.
[2] The details of sections of the law have not been annotated. In general these refer to:
Education Act 1944—Sections 15—30, 77. Education Reform Act 1988—Sections 6012, 84—88, Schedule I. Circular 3/89—Section X, Annexe D.
[3] HMSO 1978.

10

WHAT HAPPENS IN RE BEYOND THE PRIMARY STAGE?

When children leave primary school for the local secondary school there are normally some changes in Religious Education although they are closely related to what is being done at the primary stage. Secondary teachers follow the same aim for RE as primary teachers but, because they are nearer to the fulfilment of the aim, and because foundations have already been built, the objectives and the approaches may differ. They should not differ totally—the superstructure of a building must suit the foundations. The secondary teacher should not 'make a fresh start' as if foundations had not been prepared. If there is little contact between teachers in primary schools and in secondary schools to work together for RE then fostering good relations ought to become a priority.

There are a number of differences between RE in a primary school and RE in a secondary school.

● **Formality.** To some extent the RE at primary level has an informal approach. It is based upon those things relevant to the children and for this reason, at least in the ILEA syllabus, the religions to be covered are not specified. There is a reference to 'various religions' and to 'various cultures and traditions' but not to specific faiths.

At secondary level the six major world religions are specified—Buddhism, Christianity, Hinduism, Islam, Judaism and Sikhism—as these are generally regarded as principal religions practised in this country. Beyond this, what is taught should be based on the school locality and the interest of the pupils, just as in the primary school. This means that some secondary stage children will look at Baha'ism, Rastafarianism and Humanism while others will not.

At primary level we have seen that there is a need to capitalize on children's own experiences and interests, filling in some of the gaps with 'contrived' RE. The strength of such an approach in terms of stimulating the interest of the children can sometimes be undermined by failure to cover the subject material adequately—despite teachers' great efforts to avoid the problem. At the secondary level this cannot be allowed to happen. Just as balances are needed in the primary school, so balances are needed in the secondary school. In this case the balance is not only across all six world religions but across two ways of learning about world religions.

Religions can be studied thematically or systematically. The thematic approach means that a theme, common to all religions, is taken so that pupils can see that there are dimensions which are present in all religions, although they are dealt with in different ways. Sometimes the themes might be narrow—for example those looked at when discussing buildings, dress or food in religion; sometimes they will be wider—when looking at teaching, worship or the effect of religion on social life.

It is not sufficient though to look at the dimensions which are common to all religions without seeing each religion as a whole, so that all the elements can be seen interacting together. A systematic study of Sikhism, for example, might look at its background, its beginning, its beliefs, ways and places of worship, the way the faith is transmitted and the ritual observances. The two approaches enable pupils to understand something of religion in general and of specific religions in more detail.

● **Specialization.** A study of religion, in depth, is possible because many RE teachers in secondary schools have undertaken specialist training. Many will have a first degree in Religious Studies or in theology in addition to their teacher training.

Specialist RE teachers, however, are in short supply. This often puts the headteacher in the position where she/he cannot sustain the RE teaching according to the Agreed Syllabus without using non-specialist help. This is sometimes given by members of the senior management team of the school or by other teachers who have a personal interest in the subject. The RE specialist then does all he/she can to brief colleagues effectively. Another approach which is sometimes used is to integrate RE, at certain stages, with other curriculum areas, so that teachers trained in other disciplines cover RE.

Overall, about 50 per cent of teachers in secondary schools are RE specialists. In the lower secondary school (1st, 2nd and 3rd years) RE is often integrated with other humanities subjects such as history, geography, English and social studies. In the upper school (4th and 5th years) it is often integrated with Personal and Social Education (sometimes called PSME because it includes Moral Education) and careers. Whether or not this really works is almost entirely dependent upon the teachers who are involved.

If the non-RE staff are willing to give RE a rightful place, with input equal to any other participating subject, and if they are willing to learn the skills of RE teaching alongside their existing skills, it can work effectively; but if this does not happen RE is often diluted and can be 'integrated out' of the school curriculum.

One of the problems which often arises is that the Agreed Syllabus puts constraints upon what can be done. A history-led study of the English medieval village obviously requires an understanding of what happened in the monastery; how the church was constructed and how Christians expressed their faith at the time. The problem is that there are very few Agreed Syllabuses which suggest such content. If a school decides to do an area of RE which is relevant to humanities, and as a result leaves undone the RE which is actually required in the syllabus, it will find itself in an illegal position. This kind of RE may be done in addition to the Agreed Syllabus, but not as a substitute for it.

Modular approaches to the curriculum

Fortunately many schools, at secondary level, are moving to the position where the curriculum is structured in units (or modules) of somewhere between 7 and 10 hours of teaching time. When this is the case within a humanities area there is room for much greater flexibility. There is room for discrete modules within each subject which will not integrate (such as reading an ordnance survey map or the teachings of the Buddha on the Eight Fold Path), as well as integrated modules (such as 'beginnings' or 'migration'—which could include religious accounts of the beginning of the world and humankind, or how migration has played its part in the spread of particular religions such as Christianity and Islam). There is, however, a further spin-off which results from the curriculum being structured in this way.

One of the problems for Religious Education within humanities is that it is not allowed to relate to other linked subject areas, such as the performing or expressive arts, home economics or science. Limited curriculum times in units begins to make it possible for RE to be paired with other subject areas for a unit of work. It is possible to look at dance or music in religion, to see how food is prepared in different religious festivals and to put scientific and religious accounts of the origins of life side-by-side. Having said this, it has to be underlined that such co-operation makes tremendous demands on teachers both in the construction and in the delivery of such courses, because new subject areas have to be understood before they can be brought together. This time is not generally provided within normal school hours, so curriculum development of this nature depends very much on the good will of teachers. This is seldom appreciated either by parents or by Government.

Aims and objectives

We have already shown the difference between primary and secondary RE in terms of 'foundation' and 'superstructure' but it is necessary to indicate exactly what this means. Clearly details will be given in an Agreed Syllabus, but what are teachers aiming for in the secondary school in general terms? The basic aim is that, by the end of the third year, at about 14 years old, each child should be 'religiously literate'.[1]

'Literacy' is a word which is now applied to a number of subject areas; we talk about 'mathematical literacy' or 'scientific literacy'. Literacy means having sufficient confidence, knowledge, understanding and skills within a subject area to be able to respond appropriately when the subject is discussed and to communicate ideas related to the subject area.

In Religious Education literacy means that a pupil is able to read and understand references to religion in books, on the radio and TV, and respond to a religious believer explaining his or her own faith with meaning. Religious literacy means that pupils will be able to express and explain their faiths to others in a way which gives meaning and aids understanding. Beyond this stage there is the further aim that the basic literacy be increased in depth and in breadth; there are always new things to learn and to understand about specific faiths by listening, reading and entering into communication. But more is involved than simply 'doing more of the same'.

Pupils will begin to learn how religion relates to other academic disciplines and will be able to distinguish between their methodology, presuppositions and approach. Pupils will begin to put religions together, so that one is viewed through the perceptions of the other, the details become clearer and concepts expanded. When Christians look at the Islamic conception of submission they are often better able to understand the teaching of Paul that they should 'present their bodies as a living sacrifice which is their spiritual worship'. When Christians look at the Qur'anic view that Jesus did not actually die on a cross but was substituted, they can reassess the importance of the crucifixion in their own faith. Pupils will begin to use criteria to evaluate religions—is this religion relevant to contemporary society? Does it give real answers to the fundamental questions of existence?

This approach, used into the 6th and 7th years, worries some believers. They fear that it could have a destructive rather than strengthening effect on faith. But this depends upon three factors: the faith itself; clearly it will not stand up to critical examination if it is flawed in any way. If a faith does not produce the dynamic for living it is best discarded anyway. This will not worry followers of the faiths which feature in the Agreed Syllabus—they would argue that their faith could stand examination! But it depends, too, upon the accuracy of information and this, of course, depends upon the professionalism of teachers and on the support of the relevant religious community. If these things are taken into account the RE in a secondary school will never prove a source of anxiety to parents or community.

Assessment

Assessment of work in the secondary school has always had a level of intensity not normally needed in the primary school. Traditionally, therefore, teachers have corrected things which are wrong—facts, spelling, punctuation and so on. They have normally given some kind of grading on a numerical 1–10 scale or a literal A-E (with + or −) scale. Such marking was never entirely satisfactory, but it gave some indication of the pupil's relative ability—in presentation, skill, content, and so on. In addition to this the teacher would make a written comment to praise or encourage the pupil, and perhaps to indicate where more work needed to be done. When such marking is conscientiously done it takes a long time. Because RE teachers in secondary schools often see a very large number of pupils in a week (unless they are saved from this by some kind of integrated studies arrangements or by the (exceptional!) double period of RE) they can sometimes get seriously overloaded with marking.

This however might change as secondary schools move towards what is called 'profiling' and 'records of achievement'. Although the National Curriculum will, through its attainment statements and attainment targets, bring primary schools somewhat into line, again things will be much more highly organized in the secondary school.

In general it can be expected that the curriculum will be broken down into manageable units of work to which the teacher will be able to attach a statement, easily understood by parents and pupils, of exactly what is expected of the unit. In short, it will incorporate a number of objectives which relate to knowledge and understanding, to skills and to attitudes and values. Pupils will know at the start of the unit what is expected of them. When the unit is completed pupil and teacher will come to an agreed statement of exactly what has been achieved in relation to each of the objectives. As a result, parents, teacher and pupil will agree on the work to be done next within the overall framework of the syllabus. Most assessment statements about achievement will be positive, co-operative and designed to point the direction for the future. They will be called formative assessments. At the end of the course a summative assessment will be drawn up to show what the child has achieved. Together with earlier statements this will provide a complete record of achievement.[2]

Outside this school assessment, pupils' progress in Religious Education may also be assessed by public examinations provided by the General Certificate of Secondary Education (GCSE) Boards which cover the country and it is likely that Standard Assessment Tasks (SATs) at key Stage 4 in the National Curriculum will involve GCSE. The Boards provide a syllabus and scheme of assessment in accordance with National Criteria. In many Voluntary (Aided) Schools with a church foundation, pupils pursue such a syllabus for the RE work in years 4 and 5 and those who wish to do the coursework sit for the final examination. In many County Schools the RE examination is taken, in theory, as an option with others alongside the Agreed Syllabus, but in practice the Agreed Syllabus is sometimes (quite illegally) forgotten if an examination course is provided. RE may also be part of other secondary school courses such as the Certificate in Pre-Vocational Education (CPVE) and the Technical and Vocational Education Initiative (TVEI).

RE department heads in a secondary school will normally have a job description. Part of that job description will require them to produce a departmental handbook which describes every aspect of the administration of RE. They may also be required to provide an annual report for the governors. Too often the work which the heads of departments do in this respect is never seen or used outside of the department and it never becomes the basis for discussion with the local primary school or with parents. There is no reason why staff in primary schools, and parents too, should not ask if such a document exists and if they might be able to see it to help them to understand how RE is taught in the secondary school. It will be a real source of encouragement to the head of RE to know that others are interested and are willing to stimulate thinking about the subject.

An overall picture of RE in secondary schools is given in a report published by the Culham Institute. This survey, entitled 'Christianity in the RE Programme', is based on a questionnaire sent to all secondary schools, and returned by 32 per cent of them. It gives an up-to-date picture of resources and teaching in secondary schools.

REFERENCES

[1] Sometimes the word 'religiate' is used to correspond to 'numerate' and 'literate'.
[2] Full details are in 'Religious Education, Assessment and the London Record of Achievement' published by the ILEA RE Teachers' Centre.

11

WHAT DOES AN LEA INSPECTOR FOR RE LOOK FOR IN PRIMARY SCHOOLS?

All Local Authority Inspectors are servants of the Local Education Authority. They are, therefore, concerned with Local Education Authority matters as well as their own personal and subject concerns.[1]

Generalists and specialists

As a result of this all Inspectors will be interested to see whether Local Authority policies are being kept—for example whether the Authority's equal opportunities policies are being operated within a school, whether the Local Authority's curriculum policies are being operated and whether these are reflected in the organization of the curriculum and the set targets. All Inspectors are interested in education in schools, in teachers and in what goes on in the school.

It would be impossible for an Inspector of any specialism not to take an interest in what is happening in the school generally—for example whether the school is welcoming to anxious parents, helping them to feel 'at home' and able to share their anxieties, whether there is a general feeling of high morale in the staffroom and among the children and, if this is lacking, whether it is possible to find out why. The Inspector will also be interested in personnel; whether the headteacher, for example, has problems which, because he/she is caught in the crossfire of so many evaluations and consumers, cannot easily be shared with colleagues within the

144

school. If she/he has other problems he/she is not likely to be 100 per cent attentive to what the Inspector has to say about RE!

It is impossible for any Inspector not to have a general role and, more often than not, a strong pastoral role too. Some RE Inspectors are appointed by authorities as 'General Inspectors with responsibility for RE' thus emphasizing the general role. In addition to standard responsibilities these Inspectors will be called on to promote and explain the Authority's policies, work with headteachers in evaluating performance, and contribute to discussions about management of the school, and so on. This means that very little time is available to deal with RE in detail. It becomes even worse when the Inspector has to include RE with history, geography, social studies, health education, etc. This situation is certainly not uncommon.

When working for one of the Merseyside LEAs I was General Adviser (an alternative name for Inspector—of which more, later) for thirty schools in one geographical area and had responsibility for six curriculum areas, one of which was RE, for the whole Authority. A recent survey by the National Foundation for Educational Research has revealed that this is not unusual. In its 1989 survey on 'Religious Education, Values and Worship' of the sixty-one advisers who replied only eight in the whole of the United Kingdom were full-time advisers with a responsibility for RE alone.[2] Authorities that employ a specialist RE Inspector without general responsibilities (as is the case in ILEA) are very few and far between. But even when such a specialist is employed it is not possible for the Inspector to remain a specialist. Because an Inspector is an employee of the Local Education Authority and by virtue of the Authorities' interest in education and schools generally the specialist Inspector inevitably has a general function.

A 'specialist' look at RE

The RE Inspector is looking for a number of things on arriving at a school.

- Do members of staff in the school really understand what RE is about in the 1990s, to the extent that they count it among the normal expectations of a school curriculum? This involves an understanding of the areas covered in the earlier parts of this book. Information is easily obtained by asking questions (for example, 'What Implicit RE is done in the school?') and analyzing the answers, by talking to children about what they have done in RE and assembly and by looking at professional books and reference material in the staffroom (and seeing if they have been opened!), and so on. This is vital because without such an understanding there cannot be a sound beginning.

● Has an understanding of RE in the 1990's been used to utilize the local Agreed Syllabus to produce a sound programme of RE within the school? A start can be made here by asking to see the school's scheme of work for RE. A suggested format is given in chapter 3 of this book. This is a legal requirement in ILEA because it is built into the Statutory Agreed Syllabus. The ILEA syllabus says:

'It is an inherent feature of the syllabus that each school devises a scheme of work implementing the aims and objectives of the Agreed Syllabus. It should be made available to the Governors of School and will need to be kept under review.'[3]

It then becomes possible to see whether the scheme of work actually meets the demands of the Agreed Syllabus. Are all of the objectives actually being fulfilled? Are the designated approaches being used? There is of course a flexibility in the development of a scheme of work: no two schools' scheme of work would normally be identical, because the children in the two schools are not identical and the scheme of work must be relevant to the children.

The next line of enquiry is therefore about the family backgrounds of the children. How many children belong to clearly identifiable faith groups? What proportion of children come from homes with no religious faith at all? How many parents feel so strongly about their beliefs that they are exercising their right of withdrawal? In the light of these family backgrounds, the resources available in the neighbourhood, and the pattern of belief present in the community the school serves, is what is being taught really relevant? The proportion of children with particular family backgrounds can change very rapidly, due to the local housing policy or dynamics within the community itself, so it is necessary to keep the scheme of work under review to maintain its relevance. So, when was the scheme of work last updated? From questions which take just a few minutes with the headteacher and by perusal of the scheme of work it is possible to obtain a very clear answer to our second question.

● The third question is the one which takes the time: given that RE is understood and that the scheme of work is appropriate, does the school actually have the resources to deliver?

Three levels of resources are necessary.

1. Human resources are provided by the teachers. Were teachers trained to teach RE so long ago that their training only involved Biblical Studies, or were they trained to teach according to the demands of the Agreed Syllabus? The answer to this is likely to be disappointing. In ILEA about one teacher in five primary schools has received training of this kind.

2. Teaching resources are necessary to support the teacher. This involves the number and range of books about religion in the school library and the number and range of books in each class book corner. It involves display materials, using charts and pictures available from the various resource agencies and a box of artefacts and objects from each religion which can be handled and enjoyed by the children.

3. Community resources involve both of the above and yet go beyond them. Are there religious buildings in the locality which children can visit? Have any arrangements been made to promote such visits? Are there people in the religious communities who are willing to come to the school and explain aspects of their beliefs and practices? Have parents been invited to contribute in this way? Are

there members of staff of a particular faith who would be willing to explain things to the children?

A note has to be made here that caution needs to be taken with a member of staff who is a member of a particular faith but is not a trained RE teacher just as caution needs to be taken with any member of a religious community. No visitors should be allowed to propagate their faith, only to explain it. Sometimes it is as hard for a teacher committed to a faith to follow the ground rules as it is for a member of the public from outside the school. The teacher, of course, has the inestimable advantage of a professional training which should limit the likelihood of a wrong approach, but it has been known for a teacher to go 'over the top', and care therefore has to be taken.

• If an Inspector finds strongly positive answers to each of these three questions and RE is understood, worked into a good scheme of work and supported by good resources, there are still other areas to look at to gain the complete picture. Given all of these things how does the RE relate to the life and other curriculum areas of the school? This is the place to look at the assembly—firmly outside curriculum time, but closely related to RE by the Education Reform Act. When RE arises naturally through the experience of children, the writing up of diaries, local events and other subject areas, is the RE opportunity capitalized on, or is the RE element frozen out in splendid isolation? For a religious person, religion permeates the whole of life; is this reflected in the school too?

Inspector or Adviser?

Having obtained the information necessary to gain an accurate picture of the state of play of RE in the school, the next major question for the Inspector is what to do with the information. It is at this point that the verbal distinction between Inspector and Adviser comes into play.

Some LEAs avoid using the term 'Inspector' because they want to emphasize that the role is supportive and professional and not

148

merely critical and evaluative. There is a distinction and it comes across in two ways.

Inspectors from central Government—HMIs—are primarily the 'ears and eyes' of Government, employed to find out what the situation is in schools, in exactly the same way as an LEA Inspector, so that Government will know how its policies are working and how to shape future polices. Except for a written report, the relationship between a school and a HMI finishes when he/she completes an inspection. Unless there are positive suggestions in the report, no actual help is given to the particular school, because the HMI's role is, primarily, to inspect and not to advise (this is not absolutely true because, as a result of what is seen, HMI promote and often support regional and national courses which are intended to meet some of the needs uncovered by the inspections).

Local Authority Inspectors, however, cannot cut themselves off from a school. If there is critical evaluation, the Local Authority Inspector is there and, if needs be, picks up the pieces. Responsibility does not end with evaluation. This is a crucial difference between HMIs and Local Authority Inspectors.

A second distinction between inspection and advice can result from the personality of an individual Inspector/Adviser. Having worked as an Inspector/Adviser in two LEAs and having met with Inspectors in a number of disciplines nationwide, it is quite clear that some Inspectors, due to their personality, find it far easier to act as an inspector rather than an adviser. The result is that some teachers do not receive the support they need from their LEA Inspector/Adviser. I personally have tended to emphasize the Adviser role in my work. In this respect I hope to do three things following an evaluation:

1. I want to ensure that teachers are given the opportunity to come to an adequate professional understanding of the nature of RE. This might involve on-the-spot teaching or explanation, or it might involve setting up a staff meeting where school-based In-Service Training (INSET) is provided to meet the need. Because the Inspector can only be in one place at a time it is not always humanly possible to do this, even though schools ask for it as part of the INSET sought through their school development plan. Advisory

149

teachers seconded from schools can help here if they are appointed, or teachers can attend a centrally provided course. A course operating from a central venue might be an effective way of reaching more schools; the problem is that it does not reach every teacher who is involved in a particular school. Beyond this it is possible for the Adviser to negotiate with local Colleges of Higher Education or education departments within the universities to set up long- or short-term courses to meet the needs of RE teachers. It is also possible for teachers to become involved in distance learning.[4]

2. I try to work with teachers in a particular school to help them to produce a school syllabus/school scheme of work which meets the demands of the Agreed Syllabus and the needs of children in the school. Sometimes this can result directly from the school-based INSET where production of the document is the end product; at other times it needs further meetings between the Inspector and staff or meetings between an advisory teacher and staff. The input from outside the school depends on whether or not the school has a member of staff who has received any professional RE training.

3. I endeavour to encourage the school to use what are often felt to be its meagre resources in the most effective way. There is always a television set in the school and most of the BBC and ITV programmes are of excellent quality and will train the teacher as well as inform pupils.[5]

The local secondary school can sometimes be persuaded to loan copies of books used to teach their pupils about world religions, and primary school teachers will often find that they provide excellent personal introductions. There will also be people who are part of the local religious communities who, after careful briefing, will be more than willing to come into school to explain what they believe and what they do. They may be professionals—leaders and administrators—but parents are also a good resource. Resources may also sometimes be borrowed from local RE centres.[6] Using such resources alongside planned purchases of books, pictures, artefacts and videos, is not providing RE on the cheap—it might be if no planned purchasing took place at all.[7]

Having said all this, resources, well-qualified teachers, well-produced schemes of work, and well-stocked resource areas do not separately, or even together, automatically provide good Religious Education. If teachers have low morale, the best tools in the world will not result in good learning experiences for children. Conversely, many teachers whose morale is high are able to teach well with minimal resources. When teachers feel valued for their work, and when they are personally fulfilled in their chosen profession, good teaching will result. It is therefore incumbent upon the Inspector/Adviser to support teachers and give recognition of their work, to keep morale high.

REFERENCES

[1] All Inspectors in ILEA, for example will be aware of the 'ILEA statement on the Curriculum, 5–16', ILEA, 1981.
[2] M Taylor, *Religious Education, Values and Worship*, NFER, 1989, p.10.
[3] ILEA Agreed Syllabus, 'Religious Education for our Children' 1st Ed, 1984, p.10.
[4] Such a package is provided by St John's College, Nottingham.
[5] There are, of course, many other programmes which are valuable to schools but the law of copyright has to be properly understood. Information Sheets can be obtained from the National Council for Educational Technology, 3 Devonshire Street, London W1N 2BA.
[6] A list of addresses of Resources Centres can be obtained from The RE Centre, St Martin's College, Lancaster LA1 3JD. It is published within a book called *The RE Directory*.
[7] The Audit Commission has looked at the role of Local Education Authority Inspectors and Advisers and has published its findings in 'Assessing Quality of Education', HMSO, 1989, (ISBN 0 11 701449 4). It makes the point that inspection and advisory work are complementary and that future appointments must involve both. Only when monitoring has taken place can proper advice and support be given; it is pointless monitoring a situation without support. The complete report gives a picture of what the teacher should expect from Inspectors/Advisers in the future.

12

WHAT IS THE FUTURE FOR RE?

We have all seen young people at the end of their secondary education who are full of promise. They seem blessed with a happy personality, good 'A' Level results, a good job with built-in support for higher education. But somewhere along the line this promise has not been fulfilled—the different support systems necessary to bring the promise to fruition did not materialize. For some reason—maybe there was lack of parental enthusiasm, illness robbed the person of drive and energy, the employer fell upon hard times and day release was not possible—the student never reached his/her potential. I feel that Religious Education is in a similar position; there is a lot of promise, but there is a need for a lot of support if the promise is to be realized.

The 'promise' arises from two areas. Despite the general consumerist approach to life which works against religion and against Religious Education, RE has a lot going for it. One area of support is in resources.

During the past ten years the number of resources for RE available to teachers in primary schools has multiplied many many times. When I wrote *RE at the Infant Stage* with a group of headteachers from Sefton LEA, we were hard put to find suitable resources of any kind and the best available came from only two major publishers. The resource list drawn up by Joanna Daykin for this book reveals the tremendous change. Despite the social climate, publishers have presumably found it profitable to produce charts, books and videos, and the broadcasting media have continued to provide excellent RE programmes.

It is common now to see good exhibitions of RE material in

primary schools with artefacts and books flanked by charts and posters as a foil to children's own work. This would have been rare ten years ago.

Many people find it hard, given the general climate of our society, to find an explanation for such activity. It is primary school teachers who have led this resurgence in RE. Having rejected 'induction-into-Christianity-via-a-diet-of-Bible-Stories', teachers have taken on the perceived need for children to learn about each others' faiths. In recognizing the change of emphasis, publishers have moved to supply the necessary material and, finding that it has been taken-up, have produced more. This is not to say that publishers have produced an excess of material because, when looking at resources in any education exhibition, RE is still poorly represented compared with other curriculum areas—but it is a great improvement.

The second area of support has been from Government. Government has made it clear in the Education Reform Act that Religious Education is an important area of the curriculum. As a basic subject it differs from National Curriculum subjects only by being compulsory for a longer time, and being locally determined and (if chosen) locally assessed. Further, the purpose of the new curriculum is to include the spiritual dimension. Section 2 of the Education Reform Act reads:

'The curriculum for a maintained school satisfies the requirements of this Section if it is a balanced and broadly based curriculum which—
(a)Promotes the spiritual, moral, cultural, mental and physical development of pupils at the school and of the society.'

If any doubt exists about Government's intention it will be removed by reading the pages of Hansard where the debates are recorded. Religious Education was bound up with the spiritual-cultural heritage of the United Kingdom. It did cause problems though. When teachers read of MP's discussing RE in a way which put the clock back thirty years and assumed that the statements made were given effect in law, large numbers of teachers prepared to opt out of RE. Only when national RE organizations and local

Advisers pointed out what the law actually said was a near-crisis averted.

To some extent Government has also put its money where its mouth is. In making provision for the in-service training of teachers, Government has made RE a 'priority' subject, which has meant that local authorities have received larger grants than usual when providing RE courses for teachers and money has been provided for training in taking assembly. It looks hopeful, therefore, for the form of multi-faith RE which has been put forward in the Education Reform Act and which has already been explained in detail in this book. RE is not, however, going to realize its potential unless there is proper support from the Government and from religious communities.

The Government and RE

At first glance this must seem like a contradiction because it has already been noted that Government has shown its support for RE in law and in prioritizing the subject for INSET purposes. Unfortunately, at the same time as doing this, Government is taking away the present support for RE, which means it cannot develop, and has even been prepared to present misleading information in order to cover itself. This might seem rather strong, and detailed explanation is needed.

In Britain there are about 20,000 primary schools with about 193,000 teachers. Of these 8,400 teachers took RE as a 'main subject' when qualifying, and if we include any RE training taken after 'A' level the number of teachers involved rises to 16,700. If we assume that 70 per cent–80 per cent of these teachers find their way into church schools, it leaves very few teachers who have any training for RE in primary schools. Overall I tend to find only one person with RE qualification in every five county primary schools—something less than 2 per cent of all primary school staff. This low figure is supported by statistics provided by Government to show how many teachers actually have responsibility for leading areas of the curriculum in primary schools.

English and related areas	46,400
History, geography and environmental studies	25,000
Mathematics	19,600
Music	18,600
PE	18,200
Science	16,700
Computer education	15,100
Art and craft	14,700
RE	12,100
Craft, design and technology	6,500

Except for craft, design and technology, which is a new subject and is rapidly expanding, RE is at the bottom of the list. Why is there such a shortage of trained RE teachers in primary schools? One reason is that there are insufficient places where RE can be taken as a main subject in a College of Higher Education. However, Government will deny this by pointing to the fact that the places, despite being reduced in number, are not filled by people wishing to take RE. So we have to ask why it is that people are not coming forward for RE.

One reason might be the consumerist attitudes in society which are so opposed to the spiritual values espoused by all religions. If this were true, however, there would be minimal interest in RE in secondary schools. The truth of the matter is that most young people are vitally interested in religion—secondary school children are part of the age group where religious conversion is most frequent. The reason why so many children do not show interest in RE lies in the fact that they are frequently taught by non-specialist teachers who fail to engage their interest—and indeed some children are taught no RE at all!

The reasons for this have already been explained. When heads and governors fail to attract a specialist RE teacher to their staff, because of teacher shortage, they have to make adjustments to 'cover' the RE. This might be done by utilizing non-specialist teachers, using teaching time of the Senior Management Team, or covering RE with other subject areas—either in humanities or in PSE. When, therefore, returns are made indicating 'shortages' of teachers, the shortage of RE teachers does not show up—but this does not mean that RE is happening and it does not mean that there is no shortage.

Government has used these misleading figures for many years despite continual representations from the Religious Education Council.[1] In December 1988 the Department of Education and Science even issued a memorandum to the Select Committee enquiring into the supply of teachers in the 1990s to say that there would be an excess of RE teachers by 1995! This was calculated on the basis that there were 7,800 teachers with RE training. However, it was forgotten that large numbers of these teachers were no longer available to be drafted back into classroom RE because they hold senior pastoral, curriculum and administrative positions in schools. Incredibly, in its plans for initial training of teachers put forward in May 1989, Government proposed to allow students training as primary school teachers to opt out of RE training if they wished to. Only after urgent representations from the religious bodies was the decision reversed in November of that year.[2]

In fact from the Government's own figures we can see that the position is far worse. The 1988 'Secondary School Survey' showed that there was a loss of 4,000 RE specialists in four years, and that curriculum time for RE had shrunk by 17 per cent over the same period from 1984 to 1988. It revealed that of those teaching RE 25 per cent had no qualification in higher education, and 57 per cent had no subsidiary qualification. A survey of the 4th- and 5th-year curriculum by HMI in 1985 showed that 40 per cent of pupils had no RE at all and the position was even worse in the sixth form.

It is difficult to understand the thinking behind such misinformation and inconsistency and not to feel extremely angry about the way the public has been misled. In religious parlance such behaviour is normally castigated as hypocrisy. While such hypocrisy exists there is little prospect of the realization of the potential of RE.

But Government responsibility goes beyond 'doctoring the

figures'. There are two other policy decisions which work directly against RE; students undertaking teacher training no longer have to include RE in their programme but can opt out; and the National Curriculum Council (unlike parallel bodies in Wales and Northern Ireland) will not give any support for RE. More generally, however, it has been pointed out earlier in the book that good learning experiences of children are related to the high morale of teachers. When teachers are keen and enthusiastic, resources become a bonus, training an extra. Yet RE teachers, along with other teachers, are suffering a crisis in morale and until this is tackled there will be little chance for improvement.

Why has morale got so low? On the one hand the problem has arisen because teachers have been overwhelmed by continual new initiatives and have been asked to deliver too much too soon. At secondary level, teachers have been coping with GCSE, with profiling and records of achievement and with the National Curriculum, while heads have also had to cope with the movement to local management of schools. At primary school level, each teacher has been faced with National Curriculum demands across the whole curriculum. Perhaps this will be repaired in time, as teachers learn to cope with new approaches, but Government has added to the existing burdens of teachers.

Having had their negotiating rights removed, having been strictly limited in financial resources to do the work they need to do, and having been devalued in terms of financial remuneration, teachers frequently feel that they are undervalued and that their worth and skills are not appreciated.[3] Worse, Government seems to be deliberately using the media to encourage parents and public to turn against teachers as a strategy to enable pay to be held down. This is the reason why so many teachers are leaving the profession. What is true of the teaching profession as a whole is also true within RE teaching.[4]

The community

Where is support for RE to come from if not from the Government? The answer has to be from the religious communities—because it will not come from people outside of these communities. Yet support for RE is limited. It is true that many Christian members of the Lords and Commons ensured, by debate, that legislation would support RE, but within RE one is often aware of the lack of support. That multi-faith RE is somehow regarded as a threat, particularly by many Christian and Muslim parents, is a possibility. Certainly the Muslim Education Trust's campaign for a withdrawal of Muslim children from receiving teaching about Christianity and its wish for Voluntary (Aided) Muslim Schools does not increase the confidence of teachers. Similarly there is a strong feeling from (usually uninformed) members of the Christian community that they do not wish their children to learn about other world religions. Even worse, there is a significant minority of Christian parents who are prepared to take their children out of the state system altogether and educate them in isolation, in independent Christian schools. Such action creates a crisis of confidence among many RE teachers. Quite apart from this I strongly believe that such action is wrong. I do understand, however, the anxieties which lead many concerned parents to take such a step.

In the first place, it *does not* work. Every year when we interview prospective teachers for RE, most volunteer to declare their faith status. Over and over again young people tell how parents isolated or 'cocooned' them within their (normally strong evangelical) Christian faith. These people go on to say that they lost their faith when they went to college or university and found a new world for which they were totally unprepared and they reacted against the influences of their childhood.

In the second place, it *should not* work. The Bible, on which such Christians base their practice, says that parents are to talk with and train their children (Deuteronomy 6). Too often placing children in a Christian school is a cop-out, a refusal to accept the responsibility of working through problems their children face in school. It is true that the Bible says believers are to be separate from the world, but it also says that they are to live and exert influence in the world like light and salt. Separation from the world is in order to prevent the water from coming into the ship, not to prevent the ship from going in the water! Christian parents and the churches to which they belong would, in my opinion, do better to supplement the RE in state schools with teaching in their homes and communities. What is true for Christians is true for believers in other faiths too.

Let us finish where we began, in the classroom. I visited a secondary school in London's East End and, by chance, dropped in on a 'duff' RE lesson. The school was planning an open night and the teacher had left asking the class to prepare materials for exhibition until the last minute. There were pupils of many different faiths, cultures and languages in the class. Each began to write in his/her own language and script—prayers, quotations from Scripture, hymns and blessings which had significance and meaning to them. After about twenty minutes there was a quiet buzz of conversation: 'What does that say?' 'What language is that?' 'Why is it important?' 'Why does it mean a lot to you?' The whole class became vibrant and alive as pupils began to share their faith. It was a moving experience and one which could never happen if Christians, Muslims, Jews . . . were all being educated in their own schools. Without the support of religious communities not only will RE cease to flourish, it will wither and die.

There are so many possibilities for RE at the primary stage. But, if RE is to have any future at all, both Government and parents must see that those possibilities are realized.

REFERENCES

[1] Religious Education Council. Chair—Dr Brian Gates, St Martin's College, Lancaster.
[2] See summary in *The Times Educational Supplement*, 17 November 1989.
[3] At the time of writing and immediately before moving to be Chairman of the Conservative Party, Baker proposed three alternatives to determine teachers' pay in the future:
● A limited form of collective bargaining
● A pay review body
● A national agreement topped up on LEA or school basis
In the meantime the Interim Advisory Committee which decides teachers' pay is still in place.
[4] The situation for primary schools is far more serious than most people

realize. 'The supply of Teachers: a National Model for the 1990s' produced by the Institute of Manpower Studies, University of Sussex, claims there will be:

- 10,000 primary teachers short by 1997
- 500,000 more primary pupils between 1991 and 2000
- Fewer younger teachers. The peak age range for teachers will move from 35–40 to 40–45

The situation is already serious in secondary schools. In a telephone survey undertaken by *The Times Educational Supplement* in November 1989 it was revealed that RE had a higher number of unqualified teaching staff than any other subject with 19.7 per cent of schools having to use such staff. Overall 26 per cent of RE tuition in secondary schools is by teachers without a post A level qualification in RE.

ACTIVITIES

- Discuss whether the approach to Moral Education in your school relates to any of the theories of ME, and whether or not it should do so.
- Write a letter to parents to try to overcome problems of conscience which lead to the withdrawal of children from RE and assembly.
- Examine the scheme of work for RE from a local secondary school. How might this influence your own programme if you were a feeder primary school?

PART THREE
Schemes and Resources

13

MODEL UNITS

The following material has been prepared by Jo Dewar, the headteacher of St Michael's CE Primary School, Sydenham, with the help of Fran Sleeman, the school's computer coordinator. Each unit contains lesson notes for topics which involve RE throughout each year of the primary phase.

They have two special characteristics. First, the approach to each unit is unified so that progression can be seen from year to year. The units contain topics to which RE contributes, although the RE input could be expanded in each case to produce an explicit RE theme. Secondly, there is a strong Christian emphasis. This is partly because the units were originally designed for a Voluntary School and partly because the writers were conscious of the place of Christianity in the Education Reform Act.

The outlines will not suit everyone, but this is not the point. The units are examples to be considered and learned from. They can be utilized only if the particular teacher in a particular school wishes to do so.

These suggestions for the seven primary school years are separate units in themselves. They may stand on their own for the specified year, without being dependant on the others.

With slight adaptations each unit can be used for any year of the primary age-range to support the specific needs of a school or class.

However, the seven units may also form a whole school approach, with each unit covering an area of Religious Education which the subsequent units may build on.

From reception level onwards the child's progression leads him or her outwards from the self. At fourth year junior level the child is able to look further than the immediate locality towards the wider horizons of the world with all its cultural and religious diversity. However, the child's perspective is still rooted in his or her own experience.

As Christianity is the religion rooted in the cultural and religious heritage of this country it will form a major part of the approach in these units. Church schools need to refer to their own Board of Education's guidelines before starting these units.

Adaptability of approach, as well as the imaginative use of any teaching materials, is essential so that programmes are tailor-made for each individual situation. The following ideas are designed to allow a flexible approach. They are not definitive answers to primary RE.

Each Local Education Authority (LEA) has its own Agreed Syllabus. Any suggestions given here should be reviewed against the background of the relevant syllabus and adapted accordingly.

The three stages shown in each unit can be spread over the three school terms if wished.

Unit 1

ALL ABOUT ME
(Suggested year—reception)

OBJECTIVES

● To develop an awareness of self and the uniqueness of each individual.
● To develop appreciation that others are also unique individuals.
● To help each child to begin to understand how each person can relate positively with others.
● To introduce children to the concept of creation and the biblical concepts of God's fatherhood of mankind.
● To help each child to begin to appreciate that there are many cultures and religions which may have differing viewpoints.

RESOURCES

● Topic books, photographs, slides, films, birth certificates, etc.
● Materials to record findings—book making, diaries, collages, etc.
There are areas of this work which need sensitivity. Some children may come from family situations that differ from the rest; from religious backgrounds which do not encourage pictorial representation of people. With perceptive and skilful handling the discussion of similarities and differences that are found in any community can have positive results.

STAGE ONE

Family trees and family albums

Children will enjoy compiling an *All About Me* book. This can

165

include name, address, school name, the child's characteristics—colour of hair, eyes, skin, size of hands, feet, height, weight etc. Other headings could include: date of birth; place of birth; likes and dislikes; my special days (this can cover festivals special to the child); my portrait; my clothes.

The uniqueness of me as part of creation

Much of this work supports the basic skills level undertaken in the reception class—learning how to write one's name, early measuring techniques etc. It also helps if children share their findings so that they get to know each other better.

STAGE TWO

My needs

This section can be introduced by a discussion of our need for food and drink, shelter, warmth and love.

The class can make models of homes and provisions, and play in a specially created home-corner. This corner can be regularly altered to display styles of homes from different cultural and religious backgrounds, by using artefacts collected within the school or contributed by the children's families.

Posters and pictures of different types of home as well as photographs or drawings of the children's homes will make an attractive wall display.

My relations

This section is designed to widen the child's concept of family to include aunts and uncles and cousins.

The class can make a news diary about visiting relatives. Get the class to look at different homes and see how people try to create a home to cater for their own special needs. This should also include a discussion of homelessness and the need to co-operate to help each other.

Look at God's provision of food, water, shelter and warmth and his love for all. More generally, encourage the class to think about people's need to share and love each other.

STAGE THREE

Creation and creativity

This is an opportunity to introduce children to the religious concepts of creation, the family, humankind and religious ideas about the fatherhood of God.

The awe and wonder of creation

The life-cycles of animals, birth, growth and death can be looked at here. The habitats of animals can be covered in this section too.

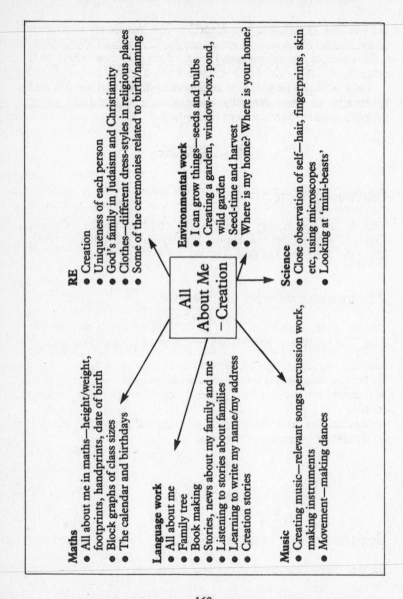

RE
- Creation
- Uniqueness of each person
- God's family in Judaism and Christianity
- Clothes—different dress-styles in religious places
- Some of the ceremonies related to birth/naming

Environmental work
- I can grow things—seeds and bulbs
- Creating a garden, window-box, pond, wild garden
- Seed-time and harvest
- Where is my home? Where is your home?

Science
- Close observation of self—hair, fingerprints, skin etc, using microscopes
- Looking at 'mini-beasts'

All About Me — Creation

Maths
- All about me in maths—height/weight, footprints, handprints, date of birth
- Block graphs of class sizes
- The calendar and birthdays

Language work
- All about me
- Family tree
- Book making
- Stories, news about my family and me
- Listening to stories about families
- Learning to write my name/my address
- Creation stories

Music
- Creating music—relevant songs percussion work, making instruments
- Movement—making dances

SEASONS OF THE YEAR
(Suggested year—middle infants)

OBJECTIVES

● To further develop a sense of awe and wonder.
● To help the children to develop a sense of the orderliness of creation in the yearly round of the seasonal calendar.
● To help each child to record something about their own special days, as well as discovering something about religious festivals of the year.

RESOURCES

● Topic books on subjects such as seasons, animal life-cycles, the year of a tree, seedtime and harvest, festivals.
● Posters, charts, and relevant slides and videos.
● Science resources—'Bug Boxes', magnifying lenses, microscopes.
● Materials for book making, leaf printing and pressing flowers.
● Textiles for collages and patterns.

STAGE ONE

Beginnings and endings

Include here a discussion of the new school year.

Calendars and how they work

This is an opportunity for the class to learn the days of the week and months of the year. They can also find out why some calendars are different from others, and that New Year may not begin in January.

New year customs

In looking at the Jewish New Year a simple explanation can be given of some of the Jewish New Year celebrations—apples and honey and wishing each other 'A sweet New Year'.

Special thanksgivings

Explain Succoth—the Feast of Tabernacles—as described in the Bible and as celebrated by Jewish people today. A Tabernacle can be built in a corner of the hall or classroom. This can be made with bean poles or bamboo poles and decorated with pictures of the relevant fruits or even with real fruit.

A discussion of Christian harvest festival and thanksgiving should include teaching about sharing with each other and the need for co-operation, as well as thanking God for providing food.

The seasons

This is an ideal time to look at the special characteristics of autumn—hibernation, migration, harvesting, preparation for the coming winter, leaf falls, nuts and fruit. Look, too, at how nature prepares for winter and how the seasons are ordered and what the names of the seasons are.

Studying the life-cycle of a tree and discussing how winter seems to be a time of death and, in particular, how some trees appear dead at this time of year will help children to understand the progression of the seasons.

Christmas and other mid-winter festivals

In studying festivals it is essential that these three elements are included:
- The historical context of the story—(for infants this would mean a simple explanation of the time when the story took place).
- The religious meaning of the story (again, for infants, at a level suitable for their age).
- The cultural customs attached to the festival.

These three elements will ensure that a balanced approach is achieved.

In approaching familiar festivals, such as Christmas, it further ensures that children begin to understand that for those who have certain beliefs, special festivals mean more than trimmings, tinsel, robins and pretty decorations.

Red letter days

The children will enjoy keeping a calendar of the year and marking in the special days in red.

As the children find out about the season's special days they can make class information books about each festival. Making separate booklets about Diwali, Channukah and Christmas helps the children to differentiate between the festivals. Young children can become very confused if care is not taken.

As thanksgiving was included earlier in the autumn term's work, as part of harvest festival, it is a useful theme to continue until the end of term; especially as thanksgiving is also an element of Diwali, Channukah and Christmas.

In discussing festivals with children, it is important to explain that for some children their beliefs mean that they celebrate festivals at different times. It can also be explained that some children may not be able to join in celebrations at all and that people have to learn to respect each other's ways (i.e., Jehovah's Witness' are forbidden to celebrate birthdays and Christmas). However, all children—whatever their religious background—can be included in a thanksgiving topic. Those children that are not able to take part in Christmas activities or other festivals can be involved in making a 'Thank you Book' or a thank you gift for someone in their own family.

STAGE TWO

Here we look again at New Year customs and develop the theme of new life.

Tree study

During the year children find it fascinating to watch the changes in a chosen tree. It is helpful to organize regular monthly close-observation studies of the tree and to record discoveries in a class diary of 'Our Tree'. With modern cameras it is easy for the children to take it in turns to take a monthly photograph of their tree. Gradually over the year the children will become very excited to note the changes in the photograph sequence. Colours, leaf formation, flowers and fruits can be catalogued as they occur. The choice of tree is, of course, important!

If the study is started in September, by January the record will begin to grow more interesting to the children. During the spring term very dramatic changes will begin to take place.

These changes will be useful when discussing some of the RE concepts that occur during this term's calendar of special days.

Trees feature in the religious symbolism of many religions. In Hinduism there are revered species of trees. In Judaism, the tree of life is an important concept.

In February, the Jewish festival of the 'Birthday of the Trees' takes place. Traditionally, when a Jewish child is born a tree is planted and when a young couple are married they stand under a canopy of entwined cedar and cypress branches.

A forest of six million fruit trees was planted after the Holocaust in memory of those who died.

The fig tree, the cross of wood, the vine and the tree of life are also part of the Christian tradition.

Young children cannot readily understand the difficult concepts involved in the Easter story, but they can appreciate the life-cycle of a tree—especially if they have recorded the wonderful changes that take place during the spring. They can understand the idea of new life if they watch a bud opening, or a flower unfurl, or watch a film of chicks hatching or even see it in real life.

Most young children will have to cope with death in their family—their Gran or Grandad, or a much loved pet. Therefore life and death are matters that they have to learn to deal with.

This part of the year's cycle can provide a valuable foundation for gaining religious insights into the ultimate questions that children need to explore. Questions such as: Who am I?; What happens when you die?; What makes a seed begin to live and grow?; Who started this world?; Who is God?/Is there a God?; might result from such study.

STAGE THREE

High days and holidays!

The class can continue recording the yearly calendar into summer.

Talk to the children about holy days and look back over the special festivals discovered in the earlier part of the school year with them. Record any others the children discover.

Looking forward to holidays

Asking questions

● What are Holidays? Holidays today usually mean travelling.

173

Look at special places for holidays and get each child to make a block graph of the places he or she will go to on holiday. Talk about other sorts of special journeys people sometimes make.

This can include looking at stories in the Bible that talk about journeys—Moses, Ruth and Naomi, Jesus going up to Jerusalem as a boy, the story of the good Samaritan.

Think about:
● Stories of God's protection.
● The story of a good neighbour.
● Stories in other faiths about pilgrimages and special journeys.

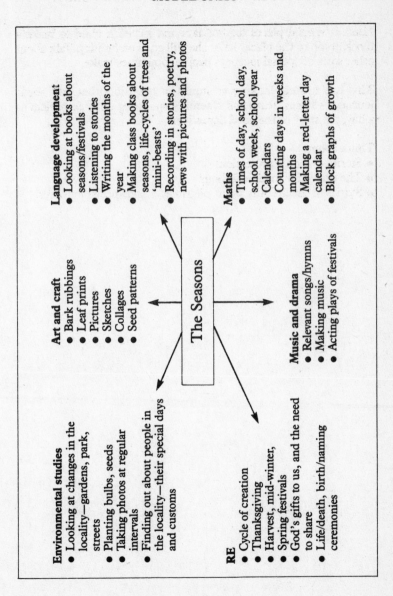

Language development
- Looking at books about seasons/festivals
- Listening to stories
- Writing the months of the year
- Making class books about seasons, life-cycles of trees and 'mini-beasts'
- Recording in stories, poetry, news with pictures and photos

Maths
- Times of day, school day, school week, school year
- Calendars
- Counting days in weeks and months
- Making a red-letter day calendar
- Block graphs of growth

Art and craft
- Bark rubbings
- Leaf prints
- Pictures
- Sketches
- Collages
- Seed patterns

The Seasons

Music and drama
- Relevant songs/hymns
- Making music
- Acting plays of festivals

Environmental studies
- Looking at changes in the locality—gardens, park, streets
- Planting bulbs, seeds
- Taking photos at regular intervals
- Finding out about people in the locality—their special days and customs

RE
- Cycle of creation
- Thanksgiving
- Harvest, mid-winter, Spring festivals
- God's gifts to us, and the need to share
- Life/death, birth/naming ceremonies

175

PEOPLE WHO HELP US
(Suggested year—top infants)

OBJECTIVES

- To widen children's understanding of community.
- To help children appreciate the need for co-operation.
- To introduce children to stories in the Bible about neighbours, caring for others and justice.
- To help children to understand that different people have different traditions and ideas.

RESOURCES

- Books about people who help us—including stories from other cultures.
- Photographs, maps, posters, charts, slides and films on themes relating to caring for others.
- Guest speakers from the community.
- Materials for recording work and book making.

STAGE ONE

My neighbours

Encourage the children to talk and write about neighbours in the class—Who sits next to me? Who lives near me?—and to make pictures of their street and town. The whole group can compile a class book of the street where the school is located.

Helping one another

Ask the class to record stories of times when someone has helped them—and when they have helped others.

It is worth reminding children, during this project, that they must not talk to strangers without parents knowing.

What makes a good neighbour?

Arrange for the class to undertake a task for a neighbour of the school or for a local caring organization. Parents could be invited to participate.

Tell the story of the good Samaritan, the story of Ruth and of Dorcas. Read other stories about people who have helped those in need.

STAGE TWO

Exploring the neighbourhood

Start by making maps together of local places where people are helped—clinics, hospitals, dentists, libraries, the town hall, churches and places of worship, lollipop crossings, pensioner's clubs . . .

Ask the children for their suggestions—they may know of places that the school is unaware of.

Get the class to find out about some of the people, places and services that help the community—doctors, health centres, the fire station and the police station.

Invite representatives of these organizations to visit the school to talk about their work or take the class to visit them.

Love your neighbour

This is a good opportunity to talk generally about loving and caring for each other.

178

STAGE THREE

Asking questions

- When were hospitals first started?
- Who started them?
- Why?

Similar questions can be asked about schools and other services. Children will discover the part that religious groups often played in this work.

Planning an ideal village or small town

This can be done by making lego or clay models of settlements. The children should be encouraged to make decisions about what ought to be in the model and where each item should be placed.

Children find this a very absorbing task and will make astute observations about the siting of roads and play areas, where people should live and what services are needed.

People Who Help Us

Environmental studies
- Making a class map of the local area, noting places: clinic, surgery, dentist, hospital, fire station, police station, library
- Asking questions: When did they begin? Who started them?
- Making an ideal place to live

Art and craft
- Models/sketches
- Painting street scenes/portraits
- Fabric pictures

RE
- God's care for us
- Christian beliefs about our care for each other, religious communities and their care for others
- Monasteries and convents—teaching, healing, helping the poor
- The story of Rahere, etc

Language development
- Information books about services—doctors, nurses, etc
- Writing down findings
- Talks from visitors
- Making documentaries of their lives in books, photos, tapes, etc

Maths
- Time—a day in the life of . . . .
- Making model towns and taking their measurements
- Estimating their areas

Music and drama
- Role-play/acting out scenes
- Related songs
- Making up songs about the people they have found out about

Audio-visuals
- Slides/films/videos/cassettes/computer programs, data-bases of information

LAWS
(Suggested year—first year juniors)

OBJECTIVES

● To help the children develop an awareness of the need to agree on how we live together.
● To examine rules and regulations that affect our lives.
● To listen to stories about laws and their making—including looking at the Romans and their influence on this country.
● To look at biblical accounts of laws—the story of Moses, Jesus and the laws of God.
● To look at the principles of other religious communities such as the five pillars of Islam and the Buddhist eight-fold path.

RESOURCES

● Highway codes, copies of By-Laws, school rules, the Ten Commandments, laws from the New Testament, food regulations, traffic rules, taboos, notices instructing people ('No Entry' etc), books, manuals, instructions, codes of practice, orders, daily routines etc.
● Materials to make replicas of Tablets, etc.
● Book making materials.

STAGE ONE

Rules and responsibilities

Organize the class at the beginning of the year with a system of class tasks and responsibilities and discuss the need for everyone to carry out their work and to respect the tasks of others. List the tasks.

Ask the class to make a set of rules designed to help them to work together more easily.

Record the rules that the children have helped to make. (Children respond very positively and contribute sensible ideas.)

Get the children to list rules in their own homes—bed times, cleaning teeth, making their own bed etc.

Look at school rules and show how they help the school to function smoothly.

Rules that affect our lives: traffic regulations; the Green Cross Code, the rules in a library, By-Laws in the park etc can be collected by the class.

Asking questions

- Why do we have rules?
- Who makes the rules?
- What would happen if we did not obey the rules?

Arrange a visit to the local town hall to find out about the kinds of rules that are needed to organize the area.

STAGE TWO

The law makers

A topic on the Romans will not only support work on New Testament times but provide valuable insights into law making.

Start by looking at the Romans' homes, towns, law and order, schools, and how they ruled their empire. In particular look at how their laws helped them to administer their lands—census, duties etc.

Study the Romans in Britain by examining their organization of roads, their villas etc, and the rules that they introduced.

Asking questions

- Were all the Roman rulers wise?
- Were all their rules good?
- What makes a wise ruler and wise rules?
- Are the laws that are in the Bible wise?

STAGE THREE

Other law makers

Tell the story of Moses set in the context of Egypt at that time and look at how the Pharaoh caused great suffering because of his lack of wisdom in ruling Egypt.

Other areas to explore:

- Look at laws that Jewish people obey.
- Look at the laws that Christians are expected to live by.
- Discuss the laws of other religions and religious communities.
- Examine rules to see if they are good.
- Tell stories of good rulers and bad rulers.
- Introduce religious ideas about the laws that should operate in God's world.
- Examine different ideas about God and his laws.
- Ask the question: Are these laws different from the laws seen all around us?

In a recent survey of the television programmes watched regularly by children it was found that the soap operas came out top. The favourites were *EastEnders*, *Dallas*, *Dynasty*, *Coronation Street*, *Flying Doctors*, but *Neighbours* was top of the poll.

Class discussions on events in these programmes is a valuable way of initiating discussion on whether the laws of the Bible are the kinds of laws that operate in life today.

Choices

Show how all people have to make choices about how they live, behave and treat others and how they allow people to treat them.

Drama work and role play linked to making choices in real life situations will help reinforce this point.

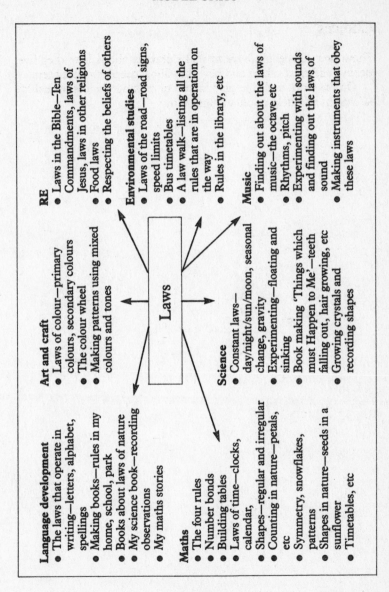

Language development
- The laws that operate in writing—letters, alphabet, spellings
- Making books—rules in my home, school, park
- Books about laws of nature
- My science book—recording observations
- My maths stories

Maths
- The four rules
- Number bonds
- Building tables
- Laws of time—clocks, calendar,
- Shapes—regular and irregular
- Counting in nature—petals, etc
- Symmetry, snowflakes, patterns
- Shapes in nature—seeds in a sunflower
- Timetables, etc

Art and craft
- Laws of colour—primary colours, secondary colours
- The colour wheel
- Making patterns using mixed colours and tones

Science
- Constant laws—day/night/sun/moon, seasonal change, gravity
- Experimenting—floating and sinking
- Book making 'Things which must Happen to Me'—teeth falling out, hair growing, etc
- Growing crystals and recording shapes

Laws

RE
- Laws in the Bible—Ten Commandments, laws of Jesus, laws in other religions
- Food laws
- Respecting the beliefs of others

Environmental studies
- Laws of the road—road signs, speed limits
- Bus timetables
- A law walk—listing all the rules that are in operation on the way
- Rules in the library, etc

Music
- Finding out about the laws of music—the octave etc
- Rhythms, pitch
- Experimenting with sounds and finding out the laws of sound
- Making instruments that obey these laws

FOOD, GLORIOUS FOOD!
Suggested year—second year juniors

OBJECTIVES

- To examine the need for food and drink.
- To make links with Health Education—healthy food for healthy bodies.
- To find out about food growth and the complexities of modern food production.
- To examine food distribution in the world and link this with an understanding of God's provision and need for fair sharing.
- To examine food laws, food taboos and special foods for special occasions.

RESOURCES

- Topic books on food and drink, collections of menus, cookery books, posters, charts, audio-visual, books on festivals and feasts.
- Information on religious symbolism of food and drink, food laws from various cultures and religions.
- Utensils and ingredients for simple cookery
- Materials and fabrics for making menu charts and books, making sewn plates of food, and for creating a café area with models of food and a cash register.

STAGE ONE

Children enjoy food! They will cheerfully write and illustrate books about their favourite food and menus. Start by organizing a café corner with menu cards, fabric meals, prices and recipes.

Class books describing food for special occasions, birthdays, weddings, Christmas and other festivals can be compiled.

In the autumn term, this work may be linked with harvest celebrations and thanksgiving.

Harvest around the world

Making a tabernacle is a good way of teaching children about Jewish harvest—Succoth or Tabernacles. They can decorate the tabernacle with pictures of the traditional fruits and find out about their meanings. They also enjoy making models of the fruits in flour and salt and painting them when hardened.

A calendar of topical food for special occasions can be made.

Asking questions

● Why are some foods eaten on certain occasions?
● What is the meaning attached to certain foods and drinks? (eg, mince pies, sweetmeats, seder food).

These discoveries can be recorded in a variety of ways.

Ways of learning about the significance of certain foods

● A project on bread and wine. The symbolism of bread and wine can be explored (bread dipped in salt, Matzos, the bread and wine of the Eucharist etc).
● A visit to a bakery could be arranged.
● Cook some simple dishes.
● Tell stories from the Bible that talk about leavened bread and yeast.
● Tell stories about food in other religious traditions.
● Look at special food prepared for winter festivals.

STAGE TWO

Farming

This section teaches children about how food is grown—seedtime and harvest and all the stages between.

A small garden area or window box can be used for simple food growing—cress, lettuces, beans.

Asking questions

- What is needed for growth?

Simple experiments with light, water and soil and planting seeds are the best way to demonstrate this.

Records can be kept of results and block graphs made of growth.

Other areas to explore

- The farmer's year.
- Weather conditions.
- What makes a seed start to grow? Who or what gives it life?
- Religious answers to these questions.
- Springtime and the beginning of new growth and life.
- Passover.
- Easter.
- The traditional foods for spring festivals.

STAGE THREE

Food production and distribution

A visit to the supermarket will reveal how much of our food is imported. A collection of food labels and packets can be examined for ingredients and the country of origin. A search can be made for food associated with religions.

Maps can be made of where the world's food is grown.

Asking questions

- How is food stored?
- Is the world's food shared fairly?

Discussions about famine and gluts raise many questions in children's minds.

This is a useful time to discuss the place of fasts in religious practice.

The Muslim Ramadan and the Eid festival may be discussed here.

Finish by looking at blessings and graces at meal times.

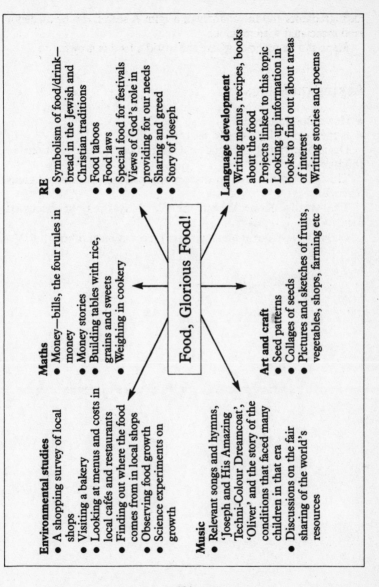

RE
- Symbolism of food/drink—bread in the Jewish and Christian traditions
- Food taboos
- Food laws
- Special food for festivals
- Views of God's role in providing for our needs
- Sharing and greed
- Story of Joseph

Maths
- Money—bills, the four rules in money
- Money stories
- Building tables with rice, grains and sweets
- Weighing in cookery

Language development
- Writing menus, recipes, books about the food
- Projects linked to this topic
- Looking up information in books to find out about areas of interest
- Writing stories and poems

Art and craft
- Seed patterns
- Collages of seeds
- Pictures and sketches of fruits, vegetables, shops, farming etc

Food, Glorious Food!

Environmental studies
- A shopping survey of local shops
- Visiting a bakery
- Looking at menus and costs in local cafés and restaurants
- Finding out where the food comes from in local shops
- Observing food growth
- Science experiments on growth

Music
- Relevant songs and hymns, 'Joseph and His Amazing Techni-Colour Dreamcoat', 'Oliver' and the story of the conditions that faced many children in that era
- Discussions on the fair sharing of the world's resources

191

Unit 6

SIGNS AND SYMBOLS
(Suggested year—third year juniors)

OBJECTIVES

● To help children become aware of the many signs and symbols in the environment that enable people to make sense of the world.
● To help them distinguish between a sign and a symbol.
● To begin an exploration of symbolism in literature, art, religious writing, artefacts and practices.
● To examine in more detail evidence of Christian symbolism in our cultural heritage.

RESOURCES

● Books on signs and symbols, the Highway Code, road signs, flags and banners, heraldry, badges, maps and atlases, coins, codes and ciphers, post codes etc.
● Places in the locality where it is possible to see symbols in use— eg, the local Post Office and sorting office, places of worship, main roads.
● Information books on religious symbolism in various religious traditions.
● Slides, videos, films, artefacts of religious traditions.
● Materials for making personal banners, fabrics for a symbol patchwork.
● Book making materials for producing individual and class books, and for recording findings.
● Clay for a clay tile panel of selected symbols.

STAGE ONE

This section is divided into four main areas or activities.

● Exploring the school and local environment for signs and symbols.

● Listing and classifying the discoveries.

● Making individual banners. Having explored signs and symbols in the locality the children will be sufficiently aware of the concept of symbol to be able to produce some symbols that relate to them personally. (If this work is attempted before exploring the locality it could prove difficult for children to make a success of the project.)

The banner may include symbols that stand for some of the child's own activities, interests and talents eg, a clef sign to show the child is involved in some musical activity, a badge of an organization attended, some number signs to show the child enjoys maths etc.

The banners may be produced on paper, card or in fabrics. If the size is approximately A3, a set of class banners can be impressively displayed in the classroom hung from the ceiling.

The children may then explain to each other the meanings of the symbols in their own personal banner.

● Understanding symbolism. This foundation work is very helpful when transferring attention back to more complex concepts of symbolism.

Looking at flags, badges and map symbols follows on well from this work.

At this stage a simple introduction to a few religious symbols and discussion of their meaning is sufficient.

There are so many religious symbols that it could be confusing for the children to be introduced to too many at this stage.

Record findings in a variety of media.

STAGE TWO

Introducing familiar objects and exploring their use in symbolism

Get the class to look at colour in environmental signs, in religious traditions, clothes, symbols and then make a calendar of the year in the colours used in the Christian tradition.

Look at the colours used by different religious traditions to symbolise a special rite of passage—colours of wedding clothes, birth, mourning, and the symbolism of bread, water, light, elements, the tree and the vine. In this work it is helpful for the class to be divided into groups and for each group to concentrate on one aspect. This will avoid confusion. When the work is completed each group will be able to share their findings with the rest of the class, or school, and put their work on display.

Introduce the class to some Bible stories that incorporate symbolic meanings—the parables, for example.

The message of Luke 2:12 in the New Testament ('And this shall be a sign unto you') could also be discussed.

Explore the differences between signs and symbols.

Look at the use of symbolism in some well known children's stories.

Visit an art gallery and examine certain paintings, looking for symbols. Whistler paintings (the symbol of the butterfly) and many of the Pre-Raphaelite paintings are good examples. Or, if a visit is not possible, look at prints of the paintings. At the end of stage two make a thorough revision of the work covered so far.

STAGE THREE

Religious symbols

This section takes a more detailed look at religious symbolism. To avoid great confusion, it is helpful for the class to concentrate on one tradition for in-depth study. As the Christian tradition is part of our cultural heritage, and its symbolism permeates our society, it would seem wise to concentrate on this.

A revision of the place of colour, light, bread and wine in the Christian tradition could usefully be carried out at this point.

Organize class visits to local churches or to a cathedral to look for evidence of symbolism.

Looking at religious myths and legends and examining religious art for symbolic meaning can also be included in this section.

Having spent some time on this work, and assessed that the children are confident in their knowledge of this area, divide the class into groups and set each group the task of exploring religious symbols in other religious traditions.

In this way each group will access information from one area, thus reducing confusion. It is better to build knowledge in one area rather than gain sketchy and confused knowledge of several areas.

At the end of the project each group should share their findings with the others, thereby introducing the rest of the class to new areas to be explored in the future.

This project gives great scope for setting up a striking school exhibition based on the findings. The exhibition can include banners, flags and artwork, and display corners of figures wearing traditional costume. Artefacts used in various religious traditions, a fabric colour wheel, a patchwork of symbols and an audio-visual display of selected resources may also be included.

Signs and Symbols

RE
- Looking at symbols in local places, finding out their use and meanings
- Looking at biblical stories that have symbolic meanings
- Religious symbolism in Christianity
- Religious symbolism in other traditions
- Religious use of symbolism of colour, light, fire, water, air, earth, geometric shapes, words, nature etc

Language development
- Letters and sounds as symbols—codes in VR, making coded stories
- Listening to stories with symbolic meanings—examining their meanings
- Making up stories with hidden meanings
- Anagrams and word puzzles
- Making books, recording findings

Music
- Musical symbols
- Making a story with sounds representing meanings

Art and craft
- Making banners, flags, sketching and painting symbols, geometric shapes in symbols
- Making a colour wheel of symbolic colours
- Patchworks with appliquéd symbols
- Making picture books of the symbols for each of the major world religions

Environmental studies
- An environmental study of the locality, including listing all evidences of codes, signs, symbols, and discovering meanings, and uses
- Using maps and atlases and finding symbols
- Examining local badges and shields
- Codes and symbols on food packets etc
- Visiting local places that use symbols, eg sorting office, Post Office, banks etc
- Recording findings

Maths
- Number signs
- The story of Adelard and the Cipher (a history of maths story)
- Geometric shapes and their use in symbolism

197

SPECIAL PLACES
AND PLACES OF WORSHIP
(Suggested year—fourth year juniors)

OBJECTIVES

● To help children to understand that some places are considered special by some people.
● To find out about religious places of worship and discover some of the special meanings these places have for the people who use them.
● To introduce children to the concept of pilgrimage.

RESOURCES

● Topic books about various places that, over the centuries, have been regarded as special e.g., Stonehenge, cathedrals, Jerusalem etc.
● Maps and atlases.
● Holiday brochures and tourist guides.
● Slides, videos, films, photos and posters of places of interest.
● Information books and packs about places of worship.

STAGE ONE

If you ask a group of children if they have certain places that are special to them, you will usually get a surprisingly positive response. It may be just a box where favourite belongings are stored, or a corner of the garden where a rough den or camp has been made. It may be a place where a group of friends have their club, or even a memory of a past visit to a special place. Most children understand that certain places can provoke a sense of awe or excitement and memories that last a long time.

Before beginning a study of special places it is helpful to draw upon the child's own understanding of what a special place is.

A class book can be made of the children's own experiences. The class can create their own special place. On a school journey, or on a day out, most children will enjoy building a shelter in a wooded area. Collecting branches and dry leaves for cover, building a shelter against a tree and eating a packed lunch inside the den provides children with all the ingredients needed to develop a true appreciation of a special place. An understanding of places that are special to other people may be built on this foundation. This can then lead on to a meaningful study of places used for worship.

Further activities may include listening to stories about secret places, places which are reputed to be unusual, as well as finding out about places in the Bible which had special meaning for certain people.

STAGE TWO

Introduce this stage by:

● Examining in detail plans, photos, slides and pictures of places of worship and discovering some of the religious beliefs and ideas of the people who use the buildings.

● Watching videos and/or seeing slides of the interiors of the buildings. This will prepare the children for any subsequent visits.

● Learning the vocabulary used to describe some of the areas inside the buildings. Again this will help the children as they access information from books and articles.

Olivia Bennett in her book *Buildings* (in the *Exploring Religions* series) says 'Thinking about buildings really means thinking about people because people give buildings their purpose.'

Places of worship are designed to suit the religious purposes of the people who worship there. Studying these buildings reveals much about the beliefs and ideas of the worshippers. Detailed planning and preparatory work is essential if a visit to a place of worship is to be a meaningful and educational experience.

A preliminary visit should be made to check all the practical details and extra thought should be given to those areas which could cause offence to worshippers. Footwear, head coverings and dress must be appropriate for the occasion.

Routes and barriers

In walking around any building, or from one place to another, we follow the routes which lead to our destination. Routes have a purpose, helping us to reach a destination.

A route may be simple, leading you from the sitting room to the kitchen when you are hungry. It may take you to the dentist when toothache is raging! It may be an exciting route that takes you to a holiday destination. Routes have purpose.

A study of the routes within any building can help us gain insight into what goes on in that building. Examining routes can reveal a great deal about areas of importance in that place.

Before visiting a place of worship, it is helpful for the children to study routes they are already familiar with—routes inside their own home from room to room, out to the garden etc. This builds the concept that routes link places that are important to the user.

Further explorations can include the routes from home to school, to the main road, to the shops, to holiday destinations, to the school journey centre.

Asking questions

- Where does this route begin and where does it end?
- Who uses this route?
- What is the purpose of this route?
- Is this route important?
- Who is this route important to?

Maps and models may be made of some of the selected routes.

The next step is to consider any barriers that might be met along the way.

These barriers include: steps, railings, ropes, doors, word

barriers such as 'No Entry!' 'Stop!', and visual barriers such as walls, screens, curtains.

When a barrier stops our route it is, in effect, saying 'Stop here and consider what happens next.'

Looking at pictures and models of a church interior

Encourage the class to examine the pictures and models to see if they can discover any routes. They will find aisles or pathways.

If the children then examine where the aisle begins and ends they will find that the aisle ends in a place important for the worshippers in that building. The communion table, altar, sanctuary, choir screen, side chapel, vestry, will be discovered at the end of the routes in most parish churches.

Barriers

Ask the children if they can see any barriers (screens, steps, ropes) in the model or picture of the church.

If so what are these barriers telling people?

The children will discover that each barrier highlights something of importance to the people who use that building.

Organize a class visit to a local church or cathedral to examine, in detail, the routes and barriers in the building.

Record these details in maps and pictures and encourage the children to find out the significance of the special areas that they highlight. The class can also learn the specific vocabulary needed to describe the special features.

Follow-up work can include making books, models and fabric records of these discoveries,

STAGE THREE

Visiting the places of worship of other denominations and religions will help the children to note similarities and differences between these and the churches they have visited in stage two.

Help the class to examine the routes and barriers that exist in these buildings and to discover their significance for the people who use the building.

The class can then record their findings in a variety of media—models, clay, paintings, writing, sketches, textiles and collages.

Pilgrimages

Consider, with the group, the concept of pilgrimage as a special route leading to a place of great significance for the pilgrim. Listening to stories about pilgrimages and pilgrims will help the children to learn about the places pilgrims consider as special and what makes them special.

Finding out about pilgrimage in different religious traditions—to the Ganges, Jerusalem, Lourdes, Canterbury, Makka, Amritsar etc—is also important.

The class will enjoy dressing up as pilgrims and acting out a pilgrimage.

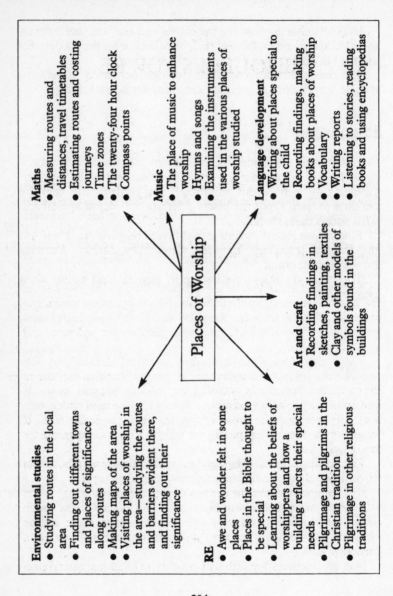

Maths
- Measuring routes and distances, travel timetables
- Estimating routes and costing journeys
- Time zones
- The twenty-four hour clock
- Compass points

Music
- The place of music to enhance worship
- Hymns and songs
- Examining the instruments used in the various places of worship studied

Language development
- Writing about places special to the child
- Recording findings, making books about places of worship
- Vocabulary
- Writing reports
- Listening to stories, reading books and using encyclopedias

Places of Worship

Art and craft
- Recording findings in sketches, painting, textiles
- Clay and other models of symbols found in the buildings

Environmental studies
- Studying routes in the local area
- Finding out different towns and places of significance along routes
- Making maps of the area
- Visiting places of worship in the area—studying the routes and barriers evident there, and finding out their significance

RE
- Awe and wonder felt in some places
- Places in the Bible thought to be special
- Learning about the beliefs of worshippers and how a building reflects their special needs
- Pilgrimage and pilgrims in the Christian tradition
- Pilgrimage in other religious traditions

204

14

RESOURCES FOR RE

There are now many resources available to teachers to support Religious Education in the primary school. Many of these resources are so good they will guide teachers who have not been trained in RE.

I am indebted to Joanna Daykin, primary advisory teacher with the ILEA RE team, for compiling the following advice on resources.

Within the last ten years there has been a major improvement in the number of resources available for RE, particularly books and posters. There is now a range of excellent, imaginative and authoritative books which are both helpful for teachers and accessible to pupils.

There is a danger, though, that increased demand for RE resources may result in a slackening of standards and an increase in stereotyping. Sometimes stereotyping occurs because space is limited in the book. For example, a family may be used which does not really represent the broad background of a particular faith. If we are aware of potential pitfalls we will be able to compensate for any deficiencies.

The language we use when giving information from a book can tell as much about the content as the words and pictures.

It is important to give the context of your information, eg, this is a Christian story/ritual/festival/object. If you do not know much about the tradition it is always wise to assume that there will be variations of culture, practice and sometimes belief within a particular faith.

Not all resources for RE will provide explicit information on religions. The book corner in a classroom will have many secular stories, on many aspects of life, that have value for RE. They can lead children to think about forgiveness, commitment, good and evil, life-cycles, communities and the world.

We can use the local religious community (and the children in school) as resources. We must, however, be careful to support the less confident or over-zealous visitor to make sure the full educational potential of their visit is gained. Likewise it is important to ensure that the children asked to help are not over-used or so shy it will cause them distress. It is equally important to avoid putting children in an awkward position regarding their faith.

In this section we will consider several series of books, posters and videos for RE with a few other one-off examples which merit attention. We will then go on to consider artefacts, how to collect and use them. A list of useful contact addresses is given at the end of the chapter. Prices of books have not been given as these may alter, but ISBN numbers have been supplied to help ordering.

BOOKS

If you have difficulty contacting publishers the Book Trust may be able to help. Their address is given at the end of the chapter.

Often the most helpful book about teaching RE is the syllabus of the Local Authority e.g., ILEA's RE syllabus, 'Religious Education for Our Children'.

The RE syllabus sets out the reasons for teaching RE and some of the means to achieving its aims. However, there are many other books which help teachers to gain an understanding of world religions and multi-faith RE.

Background guides for the teacher

W. Owen Cole and Peggy Morgan, *Six Religions in the Twentieth Century*, Stanley, Thornes and Hulton (Publishers) Ltd, Cheltenham. (ISBN 0 7175 1290 8)

W. Owen Cole, *Religion in the Multi-Faith School—A Tool for Teachers*, Stanley, Thornes and Hulton (Publishers) Ltd., Cheltenham. (ISBN 0 7175 1159 6)

The Westhill Project, *How do I teach RE?*, Stanley, Thornes and Hulton (Publishers) Ltd., Cheltenham. (ISBN 0 86158 894 0)

The World's Religions, Lion Publishing, Oxford. (ISBN 0 7459 1522 1). A comprehensive look at many religions.

Series of books

Exploring Religion Series (age 7+): *Buildings* (ISBN 0 7135 2330 1), *Signs and Symbols* (ISBN 0 7135 2329 8), *Festivals* (ISBN 0 7135 1500 7), *People* (ISBN 0 7135 2331 X), *Worship* (ISBN 0 7135 2328 X), *Writings* (ISBN 0 7135 1503 1), *Teacher's Guide* (ISBN 0 7135 2458 8), Olivia Bennett, Unwin Hyman Ltd., London. This is an extremely useful set of books, particularly for the teacher who is new to RE. The books not only detail practice of several religions but also give ideas for approaching the theme from the experience of the pupil. A teacher and pupil resource.

Religious Education Series: *Topics for the Primary School*, Longman Group Ltd, London. (ISBN 0 582 0034 2). This book is the work of the Chichester project. They have deliberately chosen a wide range of topics for the 5–7, 7–9 and 9–11 years age groups. These topics have great potential for explicit RE. There are practical suggestions at the end of each chapter. Teachers will need to develop these along imaginative lines.

Exploring a Theme Series (age 5+): *Fire, Food, Myself, Journeys, Places of Worship, Exploring Judaism, Communities*, the Christian Education Movement (CEM), Derby. CEM publishes a termly magazine, *RE Today*, for teachers looking for new ideas and information. This publication includes a useful 'Assembly File'. They also publish the *British Journal of Religious Education* which is an indispensible guide to the academic side of RE. Full details of all CEM's titles can be found in their catalogue.

Bedfordshire RE Series: *Planning Primary RE* (ISBN 090 7041 434), *Thirty Stories for Infant RE* (ISBN 090 7041 213), *Fifteen Stories for Junior RE* (ISBN 090 7041 450), *Sixty Bible Stories* (ISBN 090 7041 388), *RE in the Curriculum* (ISBN 090 7041 469), *Direct Experience* (ISBN 090 7041 485), *Collective Worship* (ISBN 090 7041 37X), *World Religions* (ISBN 090 7041 493), Teaching Media Resources Service (TMRS), Ampthill. Good, simple teacher resource books. Also available from the Religious and Moral Education Press.

What the Bible Tells Us Series (stories age 5 +), Bible Society, Swindon. Simple, inexpensive books with charming pictures and straightforward text. They are useful for storytime or assembly and are an ideal way of telling stories from the Jewish, Christian and Islamic traditions.

Talkabouts Series (stories age 6 +), Bible Society, Swindon. A smaller version of the previous series. Each book has a short introduction, putting the stories in context, and contains questions at the back. The Bible Society's catalogue has details of their large selection of Old and New Testament titles.

Celebrations Series (age 5 +): *Wedding* (ISBN 7136 3055 8), *Eid ul-Fitr* (ISBN 7176 3054 X), *Harvest Festival* (ISBN 7136 2935 5), *Brothers and Sisters* (ISBN 7176 2934 7), *New Baby* (ISBN 7176 2645 3), *Sam's Passover* (ISBN 7176 2646 1), *Dat's New Year* (ISBN 7136 2644 5), *Divali* (ISBN 7136 2643 7), A. & C. Black, London. A series full of useful information, colour photographs and ideas for activities.

Strands Series (age 5 +): *Nahda's Family* (ISBN 7136 17322), *Pavan is a Sikh* (ISBN 7136 1721 7), *Shimon, Leah and Benjamin* (ISBN 7136 1957 0), A. & C. Black, London. These are colourful books about children from various traditions.

The Story of . . . Series (age 7+): *The Story of the Jews* (ISBN 0521 31580 8), *The Story of the Christians* (ISBN 0521 31748 7), *The Story of the Hindus* (ISBN 0521 26900 8), *The Story of Islam* (ISBN 0521 27174 6), Cambridge University Press, Cambridge.

The Way We Live Series (age 5+): *Chinese Festival, Happy New Year, Carnival, Bobbi's New Year* (Sikh), *Holi: Hindu Festival of Spring,* Hamish Hamilton Limited, London. (ISBN for set 0251 00519 1).

Weddings and Celebrations Series: *Sikh Weddings, Mazol-Tov: A Jewish Wedding, Wedding Time* (Muslim), *Colin's Baptism, Kate's Party,* Hamish Hamilton Limited, London. (ISBN for set 0241 00519 1). Also available in this series: *Dance of Shiva* (ISBN 0241 10420 3), *Kikar's Drum* (ISBN 0241 11235 4), *A Busy Weekend* (ISBN 0241 11251 6), *Matza and Bitter Herbs* (ISBN 0241 11377 6), *Gifts and Almonds* (ISBN 0241 10422 X), *Sweet Tooth Sunil* (ISBN 0241 11201 X), *A Present for Mum* (ISBN 0241 10552 8), *Wedding Day* (ISBN 0241 10552 8).

Minority Group Support Service Materials, Coventry Education Authority. Write to Coventry Education Authority for details of these materials. Among the titles is *How a Hindu Prays.* These books are written in a simple style which makes them suitable for many different ability groups.

My Belief Series (age 7+): *I am a Jew* (ISBN 0 86313 139 5), *I am a Sikh* (ISBN 0 86313 147 6), *I am a Muslim* (ISBN 0 86313 138 7), *I am a Hindu* (ISBN 0 86313 168 9), *I am a Greek Orthodox* (ISBN 0 86313 259 6), *I am a Roman Catholic* (ISBN 0 86313 258 8), *I am a Buddhist* (ISBN 0 86313 261 8), *I am a Rastafarian* (ISBN 0 86313 260 X), *I am an Anglican* (ISBN 0 86313 427 0), *I am a Pentecostal* (ISBN 0 86313 428 9), Franklin Watts, London. A lovely set of books illustrated throughout with colour photos showing a faith through the eyes of a child.

Our Culture Series (age 6+): *Buddhist* (ISBN 0 86313 674 5), *Hindu* (ISBN 0 86313 672 9), *Jewish* (ISBN 0 86313 670 2), *Muslim*

(ISBN 0 86313 673 7), *Rastafarian* (ISBN 0 86313 675 3), *Sikh* (ISBN 0 86313 671 0), Franklin Watts, London. A simpler version of the My Belief Series. Beware of over generalising when using simplified texts of this kind.

My Class Series (age 5 +): *My Class at Divali* (ISBN 0 86313 425 4), *My Class at Christmas* (ISBN 0 86313 446 7), *My Class at Harvest Festival* (ISBN 0 86313 426 2), Franklin Watts, London. Useful stimulus material for classroom discussion and class activities at these festival times.

Meeting with Religious Groups Series: *Visiting an Anglican Church* (ISBN 0 7188 2469 5), *Visiting a Community Church* (ISBN 0 7188 2471 7), *Visiting a Methodist Church* (ISBN 0 7188 2571 3), *Visiting a Mosque* (ISBN 0 7188 2574 8), *Visiting a Roman Catholic Church* (ISBN 0 7188 2470 9), *Visiting a Salvation Army Citadel* (ISBN 0 7188 2572 1), *Visiting a Sikh Temple* (ISBN 0 7188 2472 5), *Visiting a Synagogue* (ISBN 0 7188 2573 X), Lutterworth Press, Cambridge. A useful teacher resource when planning a visit to a place of worship. The books bring out details on worship and community involvement.

Living Festivals Series (age 10 +), Religious and Moral Education Press (RMEP), Exeter. Short, colourful descriptions of the most interesting and popular festivals of the major religious faiths. The books are inexpensive, quickly read and are an extremely useful teacher resource as well as pupil book. There are currently twenty-three titles in the series including: *Advent* (ISBN 0 08 034373 2), *Chinese New Year* (ISBN 0 08 29279 8), *Holi* (ISBN 0 08 029283 6), *Shabbat* (ISBN 0 08 030616 0), *Ramadan and Id-ul-fitr* (ISBN 0 08 027876 0). The RMEP catalogue contains further details. It is also worth mentioning that the Teacher's Books contain photocopiable resource sheets.

Religions of the World Series: *The Buddhist World* (ISBN 0 08 036333 4), *The Christian World* (ISBN 0 08 036334 2), *The Hindu World* (ISBN 0 08 036335 0), *The Jewish World* (ISBN 0 08 036336 9), *The Muslim World* (ISBN 0 08 036337 7), *The Sikh World* (ISBN

0 08 036339 3), *The New Religious World* (ISBN 0 08 036 338 5), Religious and Moral Education Press, Exeter. A popular and familiar series covering the main religions of the world; their history, traditions, beliefs and customs.

Stories from Religions of the World Series: *Stories from the Christian World* (ISBN 0 08 036361 X), *Stories from the Hindu World* (ISBN 0 08 037072 1), *Stories from the Jewish World* (ISBN 0 08 037073 X), *Stories from the Muslim World* (ISBN 0 08 037074 8), *Stories from the Sikh World* (ISBN 0 08 037075 6), Religious and Moral Education Press, Exeter. A delightful set of books containing beautifully illustrated short stories. Modern and traditional stories are included. These are suitable for children to read or for reading aloud. The stories touch on many themes and will be useful for enriching topic work. See RMEP catalogue for further details.

Words and Pictures Series: *Christianity in Words and Pictures* (ISBN 0 08 027890 6), *Judaism in Words and Pictures* (ISBN 0 08 031778 2), *Islam in Words and Pictures* (ISBN 0 08 026428 X), *Sikhism in Words and Pictures* (ISBN 0 08 026428 X), Religious and Moral Education Press, Exeter. These are comprehensive information books with labelled pictures and interesting text. A pupil and teacher resource.

Families and Faith Series: *A Christian Family in Britain* (ISBN 0 08 0297 6), *A Hindu Family in Britain* (ISBN 0 08 031782 0), *A Jewish Family in Britain* (ISBN 0 08 027888 4), *A Muslim Family in Britain* (ISBN 0 08 022884 4), *A Sikh Family in Britain* (ISBN 0 08 031780 4), Religious and Moral Education Press, Exeter. This series is well worth reading—each book makes you feel part of the family!

Cartoon Stories from India Series: *Dasha Avatar* (ISBN 0 991340 0), *Tales of Hanuman* (ISBN 0 991330 005), *The Ramayana* (ISBN 0 991370 007), *Tales from the Mahabhtara* (ISBN 0 991350 006), *The Sons of Shiva* (ISBN 0 991360 001), *Tales of Buddha* (ISBN 0 991390 008), Religious and Moral Education Press, Exeter. This series of religious stories in cartoon form provides a lively and attractive introduction to Hinduism and Buddhism.

211

Faith in Action Series, Religious and Moral Education Press, Exeter. A series of thirty-eight short biographies about unselfish actions of lasting value. Many well known figures are featured in the series—e.g. *I Wish He Was Black—The Story of Trevor Huddleston, Someone to Talk to—The Story of Chad Varah and The Samaritans.* Generally the books are designed to show the effect Christian motivation can have on people's lives. Refer to RMEP's catalogue for further details.

Bible Stories and Cassettes Series: *David and Goliath* (ISBN 0 08 036031 9), *Noah and the Ark* (ISBN 0 08 036032 7), *Daniel in the Lions' Den* (ISBN 0 08 036033 5), *Jonah and the Great Fish* (ISBN 0 08 036034 3), Religious and Moral Education Press, Exeter. A well illustrated, amusingly told, inexpensive series of books and cassettes.

The Westhill Project Series (age 5–16): *Christians 1*, 5–7 years (ISBN 0 86158 694 8), *Christians 2*, 8–10 years (ISBN 0 86158 659 6), *Christians 3*, 11–13 years (ISBN 0 86158 696 4), *Christians 4*, 14–16 years (ISBN 0 86158 697 2), *Christians—Photopack* (ISBN 0 86158 896 7), *Christianity—Teacher's Manual* (ISBN 0 86158 895 9), *Muslims 1*, 7–8 years (ISBN 1 85234 073 8), *Muslims 2*, 9–10 years (ISBN 1 85234 074 6) *Muslims 3*, 11–13 years (ISBN 1 85234 075 4), *Muslims 4*, 14–16 years (ISBN 1 871402 17 4), *Muslims—Photopack* (ISBN 1 85234 072 X), *Islam—Teacher's Manual* (ISBN 1 8524 071 1), Stanley, Thornes and Hulton (Publishers) Ltd, Cheltenham.

These books are the result of the work of the Westhill Project. The primary levels are covered by books 1 and 2. The teachers' books are very useful and the sets of large photos, though quite expensive, are well worth purchasing. This is an excellent series containing a good selection of drawings and photos. Suitable for teacher and pupil reference.

Religious Topics Series (age 8+): *Birth Customs* (ISBN 0 85078 717 3), *Death Customs* (ISBN 0 85078 719 X), *Family Life* (ISBN 0 85078 772 6), *Feasting and Fasting* (ISBN 0 85078769 6), *The History of Religions* (ISBN 1 85210 287 X), *Holy Books* (ISBN 0 85078 770 X), *Initiation Rites* (ISBN 0 85078 767 X), *Marriage*

Customs (ISBN 0 85078 718 1), *Pilgrimage* (ISBN 0 85078 768 8), *Religious Art* (ISBN 0 85078 773 4), *Religious Beliefs* (ISBN 0 85210 041 9), *Religious Buildings* (ISBN 0 85007 8952 4), *Religious Dress* (ISBN 0 85078 7750), *Religious Festivals* (ISBN 0 85078 951 6), *Religious Food* (ISBN 1 85210 039 7), *Religious Services* (ISBN 0 85078 771 8), *Religious Symbols* (ISBN 1 85210 040 0), *Religious Teachers and Prophets* (ISBN 0 85078 774 2), Wayland (Publishers) Ltd, Brighton.

A very useful set of books with simple text and colour photos—highly recommended. The books are designed to give as much information as possible in a small space and the author is careful to try to avoid generalisations. They will help teachers in their planning for RE as they give the religious aspect of many of the topics studied in the classroom. Look out for new titles.

Religions of the World Series (age 10 +): *Buddhism* (ISBN 0 85078 722 X), *Christianity* (ISBN 0 85078 686 X), *Hinduism* (ISBN 0 85078 687 8), *Islam* (ISBN 0 85078 688 6), *Judaism* (ISBN 0 85078 689 4), *Sikhism* (ISBN 0 85078 723 8), Wayland (Publishers) Ltd, Brighton.

Religious Stories Series (age 6 +): *Buddhist Stories* (ISBN 0 85078 864 1), *Chinese Stories* (ISBN 0 85078 886 2), *Creation Stories* (ISBN 0 85078 905 2), *Guru Nanak and the Sikh Gurus* (ISBN 0 85078 906 0), *Hindu Stories* (ISBN 0 85078 863 3), *The Life of Buddha* (ISBN 0 85078 903 6), *The Life of Jesus* (ISBN 0 85078 865 X), *The Life of Muhammed* (ISBN 0 85078 904 4), *The Lives of the Saints* (ISBN 0 85078 885 4), *Old Testament Stories* (ISBN 0 85078 862 5), Wayland (Publishers) Ltd, Brighton. This series contains a good selection of authentic stories from religious traditions. The books are well illustrated with colour artwork.

Festivals Series (age 10 +): *Buddhist Festivals* (ISBN 0 85078 572 3), *Carnival* (ISBN 1 85201 019 2), *Christmas* (ISBN 0 85078 451 4), *Commemorative Festivals* (ISBN 0 85210 018 4), *Easter* (ISBN 0 85078 451 4), *Hallowe'en* (ISBN 0 85078 467 0), *Harvest of Thanksgiving* (ISBN 0 85078 452 2), *Hindu Festivals* (ISBN 0 85078 571 5), *Jewish Festivals* (ISBN 0 85078 558 8), *Muslim Festivals*

(ISBN 0 85078 557 X), *New Year* (ISBN 0 85078 570 7), *Sikh Festivals* (ISBN 0 85078 573 1), Wayland (Publishers) Ltd, Brighton. Do be careful when teaching about Hallowe'en not to get sidetracked into concentrating on the ghosts and spooks if you intend it to be a serious part of RE. Members of the ILEA Inspectorate have cautioned against teaching on Hallowe'en at all.

Celebrations Series (age 7+), Wayland (Publishers) Ltd, Brighton. This is an easy-reading version of the Festivals Series.

Great Lives Series (age 9+): *Anne Frank* (ISBN 0 85078 564 2), *Ghandhi* (ISBN 0 85078 888 9), *Joan of Arc* (ISBN 1 85210 170 9), *Martin Luther King* (ISBN 0 85078 563 4), *Florence Nightingale* (ISBN 0 85078 858 7), *Mother Teresa* (ISBN 0 85078 598 7), Wayland (Publishers) Ltd, Brighton. This is a very good series which includes several titles which are particularly relevant to RE.

Seasonal Projects Series (age 8+): *Projects for Spring* (ISBN 1 85210 364 7), *Projects for Winter* (ISBN 1 85210 365 5), *Projects for Autumn* (ISBN 1 85210 368 X), *Projects for Christmas* (ISBN 1 85210 369 8), *Projects for Easter* (ISBN 1 85210 366 3), *Projects for Summer* (ISBN 1 85210 367 1), Wayland (Publishers) Ltd, Brighton. These activity books include religious festivals topics. Wayland publish many useful teacher/child resource books for RE. Their books cover a wide ability range and are of a consistently high standard. Many titles published by Wayland are useful when teaching implicit RE.

Religions Through Festivals Series (age 10+): *Islam* (ISBN 0 582 31786 X), *Sikhism* (ISBN 0582 31787), *Hinduism* (ISBN 0 582 31788 6), *Buddhism* (ISBN 0 582 31789 4), *Judaism* (ISBN 0 582 31790), *Christianity* (ISBN 0 582 31 791 6), Longman Group Ltd, London. Although designed for secondary schools these well illustrated books provide useful introductions for primary teachers and able juniors.

Miscellaneous books

Pat Alexander, *The Lion Children's Bible*, Lion Publishing, Oxford (ISBN 0 85648 288 9). This book is also available in a paperback edition published by Puffin Books, London.

Seklya Miyoshi, *David and Goliath*, Methuen Educational Ltd, London (ISBN 0 416 505550 3). Banchu Iguchi, *The Good Samaritan*, Methuen Educational Ltd, London (ISBN 0 416 47050 5). These books are beautiful, evocative retellings of well known stories.

Peter Dickson, *City of Gold*, Victor Gollancz Ltd., London (ISBN 0 907516 58 0). A book of Old Testament stories for children age 10+.

Maddhur Jaffrey, *Seasons of Splendour*, Pavilion Books/Michael Joseph, London (ISBN 0 907516 58 0). Tales, myths and legends of India for children age 8+.

Sharukh Husain, *Demons, Gods and Holy Men from India*, Peter Lowe, London (ISBN 0 85654 050 1). Indian myths and legends splendidly illustrated by Durga Prasad Das for children age 9+.

Leila Assam and Aisha Gouverneur, *The Life of the Prophet Muhammed*, Islamic Texts Society (ISBN 0 946621 02 0). A well written book which helps to give the feel of journey in the Prophet's story.

Living in Makkah, Religious and Moral Education Press, Exeter (ISBN 0 08 036040 8). This book contains superb photos of Makkah, the spiritual centre of Islam.

Judy Ridgeway, *Festive Occasions*, Oxford University Press, Oxford (ISBN 0 19 832730 7). This super book is full of information on many festivals with recipes for each occasion.

Avivo Paraiso and Jon Mayled, *Soul Cakes and Shish Kebabs*,

Religious and Moral Education Press, Exeter (ISBN 0 08 035097 6).
A multifaith cookbook for children age 9+.

Shinda Shauson and Anita Chowdry, *Journey with the Gods*,
Religious and Moral Education Press, Exeter (ISBN 0947679 80 4).
An introduction to some of the Hindu Gods for children age 7+.
Also available on audio cassette.

Bible and Creed, Lion Publishing, Oxford (ISBN 0 7459 1823 9).
A useful book (especially when teaching the theme 'what Christians
believe') that looks at each statement of the Christian creed and the
supporting Bible passages.

The Qur'an Basic Teachings, Islamic Foundation. Excerpts from the
Qur'an.

SHAP Calendar of Religious Festivals, Commission for Racial
Equality. This calendar is published each year—no staff room
should be without one!

Books for assembly

There are so many books for assembly that just a few are listed
below. The books listed tend to stimulate fresh thinking on the
quality of the 'school worship'; the sense of occasion, seating,
themes, 'open' songs with no overt religious origin or message,
expressions of 'community'.

John M. Hull, *The Act Unpacked*, Christian Education Movement,
Derby (ISBN 1 85100 060 7). A useful, short, academic paper on
the Education Reform Act and its implications for RE and
collective worship.

Dorothy J. Taylor, *Exploring Red Letter Days*, Lutterworth
Educational, Cambridge (ISBN 0 7188 2479 2). Themes for school
assembly.

Harry Smith, *Assemblies*, William Heinemann Ltd, London (ISBN 0 435 01830 2). This is a resource book for junior and middle schools.

Warwick Griffin, *Exploring Primary Assemblies*, Macmillan Education Ltd, Basingstoke (ISBN 0 333 36588 7). A truly stimulating and refreshing book.

Robert Fisher, *The Assembly Year*, Collins Educational, London (ISBN 0 00315400 9).

Practical Approaches (to assembly), Devon County Council, Exeter (ISBN 086114 708 1).

Bright Ideas—Assemblies, Scholastic Inc, New York (ISBN 0 590 70693 4).

Time Together, Religious and Moral Education Press, Exeter (ISBN 0 08 036036 X). A book which covers most major religions for children age 8 + .

The Infant Assembly Book, Religious and Moral Education Press, Exeter (ISBN 008 0360 297). A very broad, practical approach to assemblies for children age 4 + .

The Tinder Box Assembly Book, A. & C. Black, London (ISBN 0 7136 2169 9).

Music books for assembly

Tinder Box—66 songs for Children, A. & C. Black London (ISBN 0 7136 2170).

Come and Praise 2, BBC Enterprises Ltd, London (ISBN 0563 345810). This book includes a wide variety of songs/hymns for assembly.

Alleluya—77 Songs for Thinking People, A. & C. Black, London (ISBN 0 7136 199 7 X).

Common Ground—Songs for Christian Aid, Christian Aid, London. Excellent 'open' songs on issues of concern to us all.

Festivals, Oxford University Press, Oxford (ISBN 0 19 321285 4). Practical ideas, music and background details are provided for thirteen festivals.

POSTERS

A wide variety of excellent posters on religious practice, beliefs, art and artefacts are available from Pictorial Charts Educational Trust, 27 Kirchen Road, London, W13 0UD.

The Christian Education Movement also produces posters. Contact them for their catalogue at the address given at the end of this chapter.

It is often possible to obtain posters from religious bookshops and suppliers. Non-religious posters which reflect religious themes and concepts e.g., self-sacrifice, commitment, love can also be useful.

VIDEOS

Much of RE deals with laying foundations for understanding the religious nature of our lives. Videos help to bring RE alive for teachers as well as pupils. There are many 'secular' videos which can be used in RE, just as there are 'secular' books and posters which can be used. The videos may deal with issues such as celebration, happiness and sadness (e.g., *The Snowman*), family relationships, the community etc. There are also many good videos that deal with the more explicit side of religions and how to teach RE. These are all available for inspection/purchase, and some for hire, from Pergamon Educational Productions.

The Pergamon range of videos is featured in the Religious and Moral Education Press catalogue. Their address is given at the end of the chapter. This range also includes the videos made by CEM, the Through the Eyes of a Child series and the ILEA INSET videos.

A selection of videos is listed below. However, it is still wise to look at the catalogue to see the full range before making a choice. If your school can not afford to buy the videos you need, think about sharing the costs with another school.

The Greatest Adventure Series. Animated stories from the Bible.

Looking at Faith Series. Food and religious buildings viewed from different religious perspectives.

Through the Eyes of a Child Series. Titles include, *Hinduism through the eyes of a Hindu child*. This is an extremely good set of videos which will help children when researching aspects of faith.

World Faiths Series. Titles include, *Hajj—Pilgrimage to Mecca*.

In-Service Training Series. For example, *Foundations for RE in an Infants' Classroom*.

ARTEFACTS

One of the benefits of a school building up a religious artefact archive is the fun of collecting the different materials. There is a great sense of achievement to be had from collecting religious artefacts for children to touch, hold, feel, smell, admire, hear, try on etc. Too often we treat artefacts as exhibits and not as resource materials.

Not all religious artefacts are expensive—greetings cards, candles, wrapping paper, photos, games are easily and cheaply obtained. Imitations can be made of more expensive items. For example, a paper plate can be painted to look like the Seder plate for the Passover meal. However, pressure of time may necessitate purchasing artefacts by mail order.

Artefacts for Buddhism, Christianity, Hinduism, Islam and Sikhism can be obtained by post from Mrs C. M. Winstanley, Sacred Trinity Centre, Chapel Street, Salford, Greater Manchester, M3 7AJ.

Artefacts for Judaism are available from the Jewish Education Bureau, 8 Westcombe Avenue, Leeds, LS8 2BS.

If requested, catalogues will be supplied by both of these organizations.

It is essential that care is taken when handling religious artefacts—not just for safety, but for reasons of respect. We must always remember the significance they have for the believer and try to handle them as they would e.g., if you have a Qur'an remember to wrap it up and place it on the highest shelf in the classroom, make sure your hands are clean before opening it. Even artefacts which do not carry such observances should be handled with respect.

Artefacts for teaching RE

Christian artefacts could include: chalice and paten, crucifix, palm leaf cross, advent candle, advent calendar, crib scene.

Jewish artefacts could include: Tallith (prayer shawl), Cappell (skull cap), mini Torah scroll and Yad (pointer), Seder (Passover) plate, Hanukkah candelabrum and candles, Shofar (Ram's horn—plastic copies are available), Sabbath candlesticks.

Islamic artefacts could include: prayer carpet, Tasbir (prayer beads), Tigiyah (head cap), Eid cards, compass (Islamic), calligraphy posters, postcards of mosques.

Hindu artefacts could include: Puja tray and contents, Deva lamp, Diwali cards, picture of the 'OM' symbol, pictures/statuettes of Krishna, Shiva, Ganesh, Rama and Sita if possible, Henna powder.

Sikh artefacts could include: Kirpan (dagger), Kanga (comb), Kara (bangle), Kachs (shorts), picture or statue of Guru Nanak, a Turban length.

Buddhist artefacts could include: statue or picture of Buddha, incense.

USEFUL ADDRESSES

Book Trust, Book House, 45 East Hill, Wandsworth, London, SW18 2QZ.

Christian Education Movement, Royal Buildings, Victoria Street, Derby, DE1 1GW.

Teaching Media Resources Services (TMRS), Russell House, 14 Dunstable Street, Ampthill, Beds, MK45 2JT.

Religious and Moral Education Press, Hennock Road, Exeter, Devon, EX2 4JW.

Islamic Texts Society, 7 Cavendish Avenue, Cambridge, CB1 4UP.

The Buddhist Society, 58 Eccleston Square, London, SW1. Library, Shrine room, meditation area. Can send you the Buddhist Directory and give details of Buddhist places of worship.

Board of Deputies for British Jews, Tavistock House, Woburn Place, London, WC1H 0EP. Education Office—will arrange visits, talks, etc. Jewish memorial bookshop, books, artefacts, Jewish museum.

The Hindu Centre, 39 Grafton Terrace, London, NW5. Information only.

Islamic Cultural Centre (Central Mosque), 146 Park Road, London, NW8. Visitors are welcome. School visits should be booked in advance.

The National Society's RE Centre, 23 Kensington Square, London, W8 5HN. Also at College of Ripon and York St John, Lord Mayor's Walk, York, YO3 7EX. Large collection of books and audio-visual aids.

The Sikh Missionary Society, 10 Featherstone House, Southall, Middx, UB2 5AA. The society provides free literature and advice.

Society of Friends (Quakers), Friends House, Euston Road, London, NW1 2BJ. Bookshop with posters, peace books and games.

For further information on places of worship contact your town hall information and advice service.

It is clear that many schools will find it hard to provide funds to resource RE. A few carefully chosen sets of books, some topic packs, a few artefacts and lots of posters will help. You may find that local religious organizations will give you a grant towards buying artefacts. It is also worth contacting your local teachers' centre to encourage them to start a lending library of religious books, artefacts etc.

It is important to remember that we are not limited to explicit religious information in RE so there is enormous scope for books, posters, videos, artefacts and people! RE should involve the whole person; the intellect, the senses, the body, the affective side of a person. RE should be interesting and active. I hope the resources listed will help in giving your RE excitement and breadth.